# A TREASURY OF EARLY MUSIC

## Masterworks of the Middle Ages, the Renaissance and the Baroque Era

Compiled and Edited, with Notes by

CARL PARRISH



DOVER PUBLICATIONS, INC.
Mineola, New York

*to Paul Henry Lang*



Published in Canada by General Publishing Company, Ltd., 30 Lesmill Road, Don Mills, Toronto, Ontario.

*Bibliographical Note*

This Dover edition, first published in 2000, is a complete and unabridged republication of the work originally published by W. W. Norton & Company, Inc., New York, 1958.

*International Standard Book Number: 0-486-41088-9*

Manufactured in the United States of America
Dover Publications, Inc., 31 East 2nd Street, Mineola, N.Y. 11501

# Contents

# Foreword

This anthology of fifty compositions in various forms and styles from the Middle Ages, the Renaissance, and the Baroque has been compiled in response to numerous requests for a second anthology with a similar character and scope to *Masterpieces of Music before 1750*, a book for which the present author was partly responsible. While *A Treasury of Early Music* is an independent anthology, it is also intended as a companion volume to *Masterpieces;* in fact, a criterion for the selection of pieces in the *Treasury* has been that of illustrating forms and styles of Western music other than those which appear in *Masterpieces*. From the first composition (one of a group that illustrates musical styles from each of the four great Western liturgies) to the last (a *chef-d'oeuvre* from the realm of comic opera), each piece supplies a detail in the picture of the development of European music that was not offered by the other book. When a form appears in this volume which was illustrated in the other—such as motet, madrigal, toccata, and chorale prelude—a very different aspect of that form is presented. Another difference between the two volumes, which is of lesser significance but which further emphasizes their complementary characters, is that none of the composers represented in one is found in the other. The commentaries of the *Treasury* make numerous references to pertinent compositions in *Masterpieces*.

The editorial procedure in both volumes is similar in regard to such matters as the use of short score (except where it is not feasible) and of modern clefs, as well as to barring and transposition. Also, the original note-values of those compositions that have been reduced in value are not indicated. A few of the pieces of music in the *Treasury* are published here for the first time.

The author is grateful to colleagues at Vassar College—Pilar de

Madariaga, Anthony Pellegrini, and Janet Ross—for the translations of medieval Spanish, Italian, and French texts. He is greatly indebted to George S. Dickinson, Professor Emeritus of Vassar College, for reading the manuscript and making many suggestions that have made the book better than it would otherwise have been. It is a cause of regret to the author that the circumstances of geography have prevented collaboration on this volume with John F. Ohl, with whom *Masterpieces* was compiled.

Carl Parrish

# A Treasury *of* Early Music

## ABBREVIATIONS

| | |
|---|---|
| *DdT* | *Denkmäler deutscher Tonkunst*, 1892–1931 |
| *DTÖ* | *Denkmäler der Tonkunst in Österreich*, 1894–1938 |
| *GMB* | *Geschichte der Musik in Beispielen*, ed. by Schering, Leipzig, 1931 |
| *HAM* | *Historical Anthology of Music*, ed. by Davison-Apel, Cambridge, 1946 |
| *JAMS* | *Journal of the American Musicological Society* |
| *MB* | *Musica Brittanica*, 1951– |
| *M of M* | *Masterpieces of Music Before 1750*, Parrish and Ohl, New York, 1951 |
| *MQ* | *Musical Quarterly* |
| *MR* | *Music in the Renaissance*, Reese, New York, 1954 |
| *NMM* | *Notation of Medieval Music*, Parrish, New York, 1957 |
| *SR* | *Source Readings in Music History*, ed. by Strunk, New York, 1950 |

# 1. Ambrosian Chant
## Psalmellus, *Redde Mihi,* for Quadragesima

---

The first four examples in this book form a group of chants that illustrate types of liturgical music from each of the four great Western liturgies—the Ambrosian, Mozarabic, Gallican, and Gregorian (*i.e.*, Roman). All the examples stem from early Christian times (with the probable exception of the Mozarabic example), they are all, as it happens, related to the central events of the Ecclesiastical Cycle—from Lent through the Crucifixion and Resurrection to Pentecost—and they all have a high degree of musical, historical, and liturgical interest.

The action of history brought a different fate to each of the Western liturgies, and consequently to the chants that are inherently a part of them. By the twelfth century the Roman rite had come to dominate the Western Catholic world, although the Ambrosian and Mozarabic rites continued to exist in small areas, and are still alive today. Much of the Ambrosian chant is still extant, and the manuscripts in which it is preserved are readily decipherable; what is left of the ancient Mozarabic chant exists in several manuscripts written in a kind of notation to which the key has yet to be found. The Gallican liturgy vanished, and with it the Gallican chant, except for a few pieces that were taken over into the Roman rite.

All four rites had much in common, even though they differed in details of the church calendar, certain ceremonial practices, and liturgical organization. The chants of all four rites have melodic formulas and cadences which show a distinct kinship with Byzantine melody; their common source is considered to be in the Near and Middle East. Ambrosian chants with the melismatic character of Example 1 appear to be much closer to the Oriental sources of Latin chant than do Gregorian;

and where melismatic chants with the same text and melody exist in both Ambrosian and Gregorian versions, the former are usually far more ornate and suggest a much older style.

The Ambrosian rite is named after St. Ambrose, Bishop of Milan during the last quarter of the fourth century; according to his celebrated convert, St. Augustine, he introduced hymn singing in Milan, "after the manner of the Orientals." The Ambrosian hymn was the prototype of all Latin hymnody.

The Roman and Ambrosian rites used different names for chants which occur at corresponding places in the two rites: the *Psalmellus* of this example is the equivalent of the Roman *Gradual*, the *Ingressa* corresponds to the Roman *Introit*, the *Cantus* to the *Tract*. The Psalmellus (and Verse), which comes between the Lesson and the Epistle, was an elaboration of ancient psalmody in which an entire Psalm was sung by a cantor, the choir responding after each verse with an "Amen," or similar affirmation. In the fourth and fifth centuries the verse as well as the response came to be sung melismatically, and the number of verses was reduced greatly—sometimes to only two, as in the Psalmellus and the Gradual.

The Psalmellus of Example 1 is from the Mass for the First Sunday in Quadragesima (the "fortieth"), the Latin term for Lent, in the place now occupied in the Roman rite by the Gradual *Angelis suis mandavit* ("He entrusted to his angels"). The text of this Psalmellus is from Psalm 51; the opening Response consists of verse twelve, while the following section, marked *V* ("Verse"), is the first verse. The arrangement is thus an unmistakable trace of the original character of the psalmody from which Psalmellus and Gradual evolved.

In spite of its apparently vagrant and devious course, there is a considerable degree of musical unity in the Psalmellus. This arises from such characteristically Ambrosian traits as the melodic rhyme at the ends of the various phrases, the actual repetition of long sections of melody in the whole structure (the ending of the first section from the middle of phrase four, and the second section from the middle of phrase nine), and the repetition of a motive within phrases with subtle variations (the latter half of phrase six).

The transcription is in a free rhythm which follows the usual principles of lengthening the last note of each phrase, and prolonging the notes within phrases which are followed by notes of the same pitch. The only significance of the phrase marks is to indicate ligature groups in which a note has been lengthened, and in which, therefore, not all the notes could be connected with a beam.

The translation of Psalmellus and Verse, in the King James version:

> Restore unto me the joy of thy salvation;
> and uphold me with thy free Spirit.
> Have mercy upon me, O God, according to thy loving-kindness:
> according unto the multitude of thy tender mercies blot out my transgressions.

Source: London, British Museum, *Antiphonarium Ambrosianum*, Add. Ms. 34.209, fols. 167–168.

Modern editions: *Paléographie musicale*, Vol. VI, p. 195, Solesmes, 1896. Facsimile of original manuscript, *Paléographie musicale*, Vol. V, fols. 167–168, Solesmes, 1896.

# 1. Ambrosian Chant

## Psalmellus, *Redde mihi*, for Quadragesima

7
se - cun-dum ma -
gnam
8
mi - se - ri - cor - di - am tu -
am:
9
et se - cun - dum mul - ti - tu - di - nem mi - se - ra - ti - o -
num tu - a - rum,
10
de - le i - ni - qui -
ta - tem me - am.
11

# 2. Gallican Chant
## *Improperia* of the Mass for Good Friday

This is an example of a chant (or, rather, in this case, a series of chants) which originated in the Gallican liturgy and was taken over into the Roman rite, probably in the late twelfth century. The Gallican rite goes back to the time of the fifth-century Visigothic conquest of Southern France and Northern Spain, and was so closely similar to the Spanish Mozarabic rite that the term *Hispano Gallican* is often applied to both. It submitted to a gradual process of Romanization, and disappeared after the adoption of the Roman liturgy and chant in the late eighth century, during the reign of Charlemagne.

No Gallican Missal or Gradual exists, but some Gallican chants survive in a few Gregorian liturgical books written in French monasteries. Scholars have been able to reconstruct a fairly clear picture of the Gallican Mass, one of whose fixed elements was the *Trisagion* ("thrice-blessed"), which forms part of the *Improperia* ("reproaches"). The use of the Improperia on Good Friday appears to have been part of the Gallican rite by the end of the sixth century.

The Trisagion, also called the *Agios O Theos* ("O Holy God") after the opening Greek words, is a brief hymn or invocation, and is very old; some scholars believe that it may even be of apostolic origin. The melody stems from a Byzantine version which is much simpler in structure. The Trisagion is unique in the Roman liturgy as the only place where a text is sung in both Greek and Latin; it is the last vestige of a practice that was once apparently widespread in the Middle Ages of singing certain texts in both languages on important feasts.

The Improperia are sung after the reading of the Passion (John 18, 19), the Collects, and the singing of the Antiphon *Ecce lignum crucis*

("Behold the wood of the cross"). Then begins the series of reproaches which the Saviour is made to utter against the Jews, who in return for divine favor—especially the delivery from Egypt—inflicted upon him the shame of the Passion and a bitter death. The reproaches are parts of verses from the Prophets (Micah 6:3, 4; Jeremiah 2:6, 7; Isaiah 5:2, 4), which are briefly augmented to link them to the Gospel. Each reproach is followed by the singing of the Trisagion, the third singing of which concludes the first part of the Improperia, given in Example 2. The second part, which does not appear in the example, consists of nine more reproaches in the same spirit, each of which is a Scriptural verse; each of these is followed by the *Popule meus*—the phrase with which the first part of the Improperia begins—as a sort of refrain.

The three reproaches are closely related musically; each has phrases that are heard in the others, and each ends with the same phrase. The melodic design of each individual reproach is itself strongly unified by the repetition and occasional variation of phrases and figures. The Trisagion is melodically contrasted to the reproaches; each of its three members is repeated note for note in the Latin repetition of the Greek text, and each ends with the same cadential figure.

The tragic, sombre mood of Good Friday is dramatically reflected in the rubrics of the Mass for this day, which direct that the service be carried out by the officiants in black garments, and without lights or incense; the Passion is read at a lectern stripped of all ornaments, the blessing is not asked for, nor is the book kissed after the reading.

The text, translated:

O my people, what have I done unto thee, and wherein have I wearied thee? Answer me. Because I led thee from the land of Egypt thou didst prepare the cross for thy Saviour.

O Holy God:
Holy, Strong:
Holy, Immortal, have mercy upon us.

Because I led thee through the desert for forty years, and fed thee manna, and led thee into a land of plenty, thou did'st prepare the cross for thy Saviour.

O Holy God. . . .

What more ought I to have done for thee, and did not? Yet I had planted thee a noble vine, wholly a right seed; how then have you turned degenerate and become a wild vine?

O Holy God. . . .

Source: *Liber usualis*, p. 704, Tournai, 1950.

## 2. Gallican Chant

### *Improperia* of the Mass for Good Friday

**Two Cantors sing the following in the middle of the Choir:**

℣. Po- pu - le ______ me - us, quid fe - ci ti - bi?

aut in quo ______ con - tri - sta - vi te? ______

re - spon - de mi - hi. ℣. Qui - a e - du - xi te

de ter-ra ______ Ae - gyp - ti: pa - ra - - - sti cru -

**One Choir sings:**

cem ______ Sal - va- to - ri tu - o. A - gi - os, ______

**The other Choir responds:**

______ o The - os. ______ San-ctus ______ De - us. ______

**The first Choir:** **The second Choir:**

A - gi - os ______ i - schy - ros. ______ San- ctus ______ for -

**The first Choir:**

tis. ______ A - gi - os ______ a - tha - na- tos, ______

**The second Choir:**

e - le - - i - son ______ i - mas. ______ San - ctus ______

im - mor- ta - lis, ______ mi - se - - re - re ______ no - bis. ______

Two cantors of the second Choir:
Qui - a e - du - xi te per de - ser - - tum
qua - dra - gin - ta an - nis, et man - na ci - ba - vi te,
et in - tro - du - xi in ter - ram sa - tis op - ti - mam:
pa - ra - - sti cru - cem Sal - va - to - ri tu - o.
The two choirs respond in turn: Agios o Theus, Sanctus Deus etc.
It is always the first Choir that sings Agios.
Then two Cantors of the first Choir sing:
Quid ul - tra de - bu - i fa - ce - re ti - bi, et non fe - ci?
E - - go qui - dem plan - ta - vi te vi - ne - am me -
am spe - ci - o - sis - si - mam: et tu fac - ta
es mi - hi ni - mis a - ma - ra: a - ce - to nam - que
si - tim me - am po - ta - sti: et lan - ce - a per -
fo - ra - sti la - tus Sal - va - to - ri tu - o.

The two Choirs respond again in turn: *Agios o Theus, Sanctus Deus* etc.

# 3. Mozarabic Chant

## Antiphon, *Gaudete Populi*, of the Mass for Easter

The Christian liturgy in Spain has had a strange history, and the ancient Spanish chant remains practically a closed book to us even today. Even the name given to the chant—"Mozarabic"—is unsatisfactory to many scholars; it is derived from "Mozarabs," *i.e.*, the Christians who were tolerated under Moorish rule (eighth to eleventh centuries) in Aragon, Castile, and Leon. The rite itself shows no trace of Arab influence, however. The term "Visigothic" is also applied to this rite and its chant, in reference to the conquest of Spain by the tribes that overran Northern Spain in the early fifth century; but it is probable that the chant goes back even further, for Spain was Christian before the coming of the Visigoths. The liturgy and its chant were suppressed in the eleventh century when the Roman rite was introduced into Aragon and Castile; the Mozarabic rite itself never died and is still celebrated in Toledo, but the chant has had a different history.

The suppression of the Mozarabic liturgy at the end of the eleventh century occurred at a time when neume notation which readily conveyed definite pitch indications was rapidly coming into use in Western Europe. The chants of the Mozarabic rite were not transcribed into this kind of notation by those who knew the traditional melodies; consequently, although many Mozarabic chant manuscripts still exist, the notation in which they are written has so far resisted all attempts to decipher it.

Some of these melodies lie buried in liturgical books written in the sixteenth century. At that time an effort was made to restore the Mozarabic rite; however, when the sixteenth-century scribes wrote down the melodies, they imposed on them a rythmical character that was foreign to the original form. Spanish scholars of today have restored the chant by putting the melodies back into what they consider the original rhythm to have been. Example 3 is one of these restored melodies.

*Gaudete populi* is one of eight variable chants used in the Mozarabic rite which were called *Ad accedentes* ("for the approach"), sung while the congregation approached the priest to receive the wafer; they are hence analogous to the Roman *Communion.* (Like the other Western rites, the Mozarabic differs from that of the Eastern church by having a great many parts that are variable according to the day.) *Gaudete populi* is for the Communion at Easter, and its melody is a particularly apt setting of the triumphant and joyful climax to the Easter drama. The melody itself cannot be assigned to any particular period; it is nevertheless an authentic chant of the Mozarabic rite and one of great intrinsic musical beauty. It may be classed as an Antiphon of the type which is not an enframing melody to a Psalm, but an independent chant. It is closely related in design to the psalmodic antiphon type through its recited antiphonal verses: the first two verses are followed by a response consisting of the phrase "Surrexit. . ." in the Antiphon proper; the third (final) verse is the "Gloria patri," which is followed by a return to the opening phrase of the Antiphon to round off the whole.

The text is not Biblical, but a paraphrase of the scene of the Resurrection described in the last three Gospels.

Rejoice, ye peoples, and be glad.
An angel sat upon the tomb of the Lord;
He proclaimed the glad tidings to us:
  "Christ arose from the dead;
  The Saviour of the world;
  And filled all again with sweetness."
His countenance was like light,
And his clothing like snow,
And he said:
  "Christ arose. . ."
Glory and honor to the Father and to the Son,
And to the Holy Ghost, forever and ever,
Amen.
Rejoice, ye peoples, and be glad.

Source: Dom G. Prado, O.S.B., "Mozarabic Melodics," *Speculum*, 1928, p. 218.

## 3. Mozarabic Chant

### Antiphon, *Gaudete Populi*, of the Mass for Easter

et gau - di - o ma - gno cur - ren - tes nun - ti - a - re
di - sci - pu - lis qui - a re - sur - rex - it.
First choir again sings:
*Christus resurrexit . . .*
The two choirs
Glo - ri - a et ho - nor Pa - tri et Fi - li - o, et Spi -
ri - tu - i San - cto, in sae - cu - la sae - cu - lo - rum. A - men.
Gau - de - te, po - pu - li, et ___ lae - ta - mi - ni.

# 4. Gregorian Chant
## Hymn, *Veni Creator Spiritus*, for the Second Vespers of Whitsunday

In the Roman rite the hymn is used principally in the Office, although it is prescribed in a certain few Masses. The hymn comes from the Eastern churches, where it has always figured more largely in the service than in the West. The earliest hymns in use today are from the latter fourth century, and were written by St. Ambrose (see commentary to Example 1).

*Veni Creator Spiritus* ("Come, O Creator Spirit") is the Office Hymn for the Second Vespers of Whitsunday, the English name for Pentecost, the "fiftieth" day—or seventh Sunday—after Easter. This festival commemorates the descent of the Holy Ghost upon the Apostles. The Office of Vespers, aside from the introductory and concluding prayers, consists of five Psalms with Antiphons, a short Scripture reading, the Office Hymn, and the Magnificat with Antiphon. In Second Vespers for Whitsunday the Scripture is Acts 2:1 and 2—a vivid description of the descent of the Holy Ghost—after which *Veni Creator* is sung. The same order is followed throughout the Octave of Pentecost (that is, the continued observance of this festival for eight days, Easter and Pentecost being exceptional in having seven-day "Octaves"), except that the Antiphon of the Magnificat and the Prayers are proper for each day.

*Veni Creator Spiritus* is the most famous of all Latin hymns, and has been ascribed at various times to different famous personages such as Charlemagne, St. Ambrose, and St. Gregory. However, there seems good reason to believe that the most likely author was Hrabanus Maurus, Abbot of Fulda and Archbishop of Mainz in the ninth century; the use of the hymn in the Office at Pentecost has been traced back to the tenth century. Its singing in the Middle Ages was always marked with signs of particular ceremony—the ringing of bells, the use of incense, lights, special vestments, and other signs of honor. From the eleventh century it has been used at Ordinations. In the Anglican Church it is the only hymn specifically prescribed by the Book of Common Prayer; in the rubrics for the Ordering of Priests (p. 540) it is directed that at a certain point in the liturgy "the Bishop shall sing or say the *Veni, Creator Spiritus,*" and that it be delivered responsorially between the Bishop and the others present. The *Liber usualis* has this rubric for the hymn: "All kneel for the first stanza of the following hymn."

*Veni Creator* has seven verses in iambic dimeter, the customary meter of Latin hymns, and is arranged in four-line stanzas; it has some traces of rhyme. The melody which is associated with the hymn is thought to be very much older than the hymn itself; it was also used with the Ambrosian hymn *Hic est dies verus Dei* ("This is the true day of God"). It is in the eighth mode, defined by its final (G) and the melodic emphasis given its dominant (C). The over-all arch of the lovely melody is repeated in various ways in the smaller arches within each of the four phrases of which it is comprised; melodic rhyme occurs at the cadences of phrases one, two, and four.

The hymn with its melody was widely used in the Renaissance. It would have been strange indeed if Luther had not appropriated the melody for a German chorale; a polyphonic setting of it by his musical advisor, Johann Walter, appears as Example 24 of this book: *Komm, Gott Schöpfer, heiliger Geist.* (Note also Bach's setting—No. 187 of the 371 Chorales—given at the end of the commentary to Example 24.) Heinrich Finck treated it as a *quodlibet* (a melody which combines two or more well-known melodies; see commentary to Example 31), combining it with *Veni Sancte Spiritus* (see *HAM,* No. 80). Costanzo Festa treated the various stanzas alternately in polyphony and plainsong, in the manner of Morales' *Magnificat* setting (see Example 23); and Palestrina used the melody as a tenor cantus firmus in his *Missa Veni Creator Spiritus.* English Renaissance composers apparently had a special regard for the tune: it was set by Dunstable, Tallis, Phillips, and others; and Byrd and Bull even used it in some of their pieces for the virginal, where it also appears under the title of *Salvator mundi* ("Saviour of the world"). It also appears as a polyphonic hymn in the French collection of late fourteenth-century sacred music, the *Manuscrit d'Apt* (see commentary to Example 14).

The translation of Robert Bridges in the *Yattenden Hymnal* (London, 1920) has been selected for use in this book, because of its literary quality and its faithfulness to the original.

Come, O Creator Spirit, come,
And make within our hearts thy home:
To us thy Grace celestial give,
Who of thy breathing move and live.

O Comforter, that name is thine,
Of God most high the gift divine:
The well of life, the fire of love,
Our soul's anointing from above.

Thou dost appear in sevenfold dower,
The gift of God's almighty power:
The Father's promise making rich
With saving truth our mortal speech.

Our senses with thy light inflame:
Our hearts to heav'nly love reclaim:
Our bodies' poor infirmity
With strength perpetual fortify.

Our earthly foes afar repel,
Give us henceforth in peace to dwell;
And so to us, with Thee for guide,
No ill shall come, no harm betide.

May we by Thee the Father learn,
And know the Son, and Thee discern,
Who art of both: and so adore
In perfect faith for evermore.

Stanza 7 (not included in Bridges' translation):

Glory be to the Father,
And to the Son, from death aris'n,
And to the Holy Ghost,
For ever and ever. Amen.

Source: *Liber usualis*, p. 885, Tournai, 1950.

## 4. Gregorian Chant

### Hymn, *Veni Creator Spiritus*, for the Second Vespers of Whitsunday

1. Ve - ni Cre - a - tor Spi - ri - tus, Men - tes tu - o -
2. Qui di - ce - ris Pa - ra - cli - tus, Al - tis - si - mi
3. Tu sep - ti - for - mis mu - ne - re, Di - gi - tus pa - ter -
4. Ac - cen - de lu - men sen - si - bus, In - fun - de a - mo -
5. Ho - stem re - pel - las lon - gi - us, Pa - cem - que do -
6. Per te sci - a - mus da Pa - trem, No - sca - mus at -
7. De - o Pa - tri sit glo - ri - a, Et Fi - li - o,
rum vi - si - ta: Im - ple su - per - na gra - ti - a
do - num De - i, Fons vi - vus, i - gnis, ca - ri - tas,
nae dex - te - rae, Tu ri - te pro - mis - sum Pa - tris,
rem cor - di - bus, In - fir - ma no - stri cor - po - ris
nes pro - ti - nus: Duc - to - re sic te prae - vi - o,
que Fi - li - um, Te - que u - tri - us - que Spi - ri - tum
qui a mor - tu - is Sur - re - xit, ac Pa - ra - cli - to,
Quae tu cre - a - sti pec - to - ra.
Et spi - ri - ta - lis unc - ti - o.
Ser - mo - ne di - tans gut - tu - ra.
Vir - tu - te fir - mans per - pe - ti.
Vi - te - mus om - ne no - xi - um.
Cre - da - mus om - ni tem - po - re.
In sae - cu - lo - rum sae - cu - la. A - men.

# 5. Liturgical Drama
## *Infantem Vidimus*

---

Medieval plays portraying Biblical stories and written for performance in the church exist in a number of manuscripts from the tenth to the thirteenth centuries. They are customarily referred to as "liturgical dramas," even though they were never an integral part of the liturgy. The texts of almost all these plays are in Latin, and their musical settings are written in the neume notation of plainchant. Most of them are written around the Easter and Christmas stories; but such stories as the Raising of Lazarus, the Wise and Foolish Virgins, the Last Judgment, and others from the New and Old Testaments are also treated.

The genesis of the liturgical plays has been traced to the practice of adding a short trope of three sentences before the Introit of the Mass of Easter, consisting of a brief dialogue between the Angel at the empty tomb and the three Marys come to seek the crucified body of Jesus. This is called the "Quem quaeritis" trope, after the first words with which the dialogue begins: "*Quem quaeritis in sepulchro, Christicolae?*" ("Whom seek ye in the sepulchre, ye followers of Christ?" See *GMB*, No. 8.) In the late tenth century the trope was moved to the end of Easter Matins, expanded, and presented in dramatic fashion with costumes and properties; "stage directions" for its performance are indicated in many manuscripts, the earliest of these being the Winchester Troper (late tenth century). Subsequently many additions were made to the scene which were inspired by suggestions in the Gospel account of the Resurrection, such as the episodes of the two disciples running towards the sepulchre, the meeting of Christ with the Marys, and the journey to Emmaus—the last representing a special category of the Easter play known as the *Peregrinus* ("Wanderer") plays.

The Christmas play developed in like manner to the Easter play, probably in imitation of it, as it appears somewhat later. Like the Easter play, it also derived from a trope, in this case one that paraphrases the Gospel account of the Saviour's birth and the adoration of the shepherds. The opening words of the Christmas trope are: "*Quem quaeritis in praesepe?*" ("Whom seek ye in the manger?"), an obvious echo of the Easter trope. In the later development of the Christmas play, two additional scenes appear: the Journey of the Magi, and Herod's Slaughter of the Innocents. According to a manuscript of a Christmas play in Rouen, the drama was given between Terce and Mass on Epiphany (January 6, the twelfth day after Christmas).

The music for liturgical dramas developed in somewhat the same way as the texts. At first melodies were borrowed from plainsong—either whole antiphons, hymns, and sequences, or a selection of certain plainchant formulas; these were later expanded by an increasing use of original composition. Most plays end with an appropriate liturgical chant, the most frequently used being the canticle *Te Deum laudamus* ("We praise Thee, O Lord").

*Infantem vidimus*, Example 5, which is usually referred to as The Play of the Three Kings, has been preserved in a late eleventh- or early twelfth-century manuscript from the Benedictine Monastery at Einsiedeln, Switzerland, a noted place of pilgrimage in the Middle Ages. This is a developed version of the Christmas story, with the Magi and Herod accretions; it concludes with a Hymn of the Prophets, an impressive and original composition which is unique to this manuscript. The beginning of the drama is missing; but as the text is closely similar to other manuscript versions of the Christmas play from Rouen, Orleans, Paris, and Munich, it may be assumed that the missing section is the same opening scene of the Adoration of the Shepherds which appears in these other versions.

Another lacuna of a different sort occurs in the drama itself: the words *Te Deum laudamus* are given, but no music is indicated. This phrase is the incipit of the canticle sung at the end of Nocturns or Matins, which was widely known as far back as the sixth century. Since the phrase occurs in the middle of the play, it may be that only the incipit was sung at this point, rather than the whole canticle; brackets on the staff enclose an editorial addition of the first phrase of the canticle. The manuscript directs that the Chorus sing this phrase, and also the refrain after each verse of the Prophet's Hymn at the end.

The Wise Men refer to themselves in the text as the Kings of Tharsis, Arabia, and Saba; this was probably suggested by Psalms 72:10: "The kings of Tarshish and of the isles shall bring presents: the kings of Sheba and Seba shall offer gifts". In the context of the Christmas play they thus become witnesses of the fulfillment of the prophecy.

The translation of the text follows:

*Shepherds:* We have seen the infant.

*Boys:* Who are those whom the star leads, approaching us and bearing strange things?

*Magi:* We are those whom you see—the Kings of Tharsis, Arabia, and Saba, offering gifts to Christ the King, the new-born Lord.

*Boys:* Here is the boy whom ye seek; hasten now to adore, for he is the Redemption of the world.

*Magi:* Hail, eternal King! Receive, O King, gold; accept frankincense, thou true God; and myrrh, the sign of the sepulchre!

*Angel:* Fulfilled are all those things which were spoken by the prophet. But go back by another way, for unless you inform the king you will be greatly punished.

*Magi:* O King of Heaven!

*Chorus:* We praise Thee, O God! (*Te Deum laudamus*)

*Messenger:* Deceived art thou, master: the Magi will go back by another way.

*Armor-bearer:* Resolve, O master, to avenge thy wrath, and order the boy sought out with a merciless sword; perhaps among those who are slain the boy will be slain also.

*King:* By their destruction I shall put out my flame; go, have the boys destroyed by the sword.

*Prophets:* Let us rejoice, celebrating the festival of the glorious and renowned King, proclaiming that by his birth we have given to us the haven of life.

*Chorus:* (*Repeat:* "Let us rejoice. . . .")

*Prophets:* Behold, we preach the King, the new given law of the whole world, we declare the One whose reign must be, recorded by the Prophet.

*Chorus:* (*Repeat:* "Let us rejoice. . . .")

*Prophets:* Those things which the Prophet said about the coming highest King are fulfilled, the hearts of impious Jews deny that his rule is about to be.

*Chorus:* (*Repeat:* "Let us rejoice. . . .")

*Prophets:* The people in Judea now are set apart through the royal power, and the Gentiles, formerly the vile ones, are converted by the celestial majesty.

*Chorus:* (*Repeat:* "Let us rejoice. . . .")

*Prophets:* Those confessing the true God, the King of Kings, will be saved through baptism; but those condemning the Holy King will be damned, He having been made King of Judea.

*Chorus:* (*Repeat:* "Let us rejoice. . . .")

*Prophets:* Jesse's stem is perceived to have flowered and to have given forth a new fruit to faithless Israel, He born to Mary is known to be now at hand.

*Chorus:* (*Repeat:* "Let us rejoice. . . .")

Source: Einsiedeln, *Stiftsbibliothek,* No. 367.
Modern edition: Dom P. Schubiger, O.S.B., "Das liturgische Drama des Mittelalters und seine Musik," *Musikalische Spicilegien,* p. 44, Berlin, 1876.

## 5. Liturgical Drama (11th–12th Century)

### *Infantem Vidimus*

Pastores
Pueri
In - fan - tem vi - di - mus. Qui sunt hi, quos stel - la du - cit
Magi
nos a - de - un - tes, in - au - di - ta fe - ren - tes? Nos su - mus quos
cer - ni - tes re - ges Thar - sis et A - ra - bum et Sa - ba,
do - na of - fe - ren - tes Chri - sto Re - gi na - to Do - mi - no.
Pueri
Ec - ce pu - er ad - est quem quae - ri - tis, jam pro - pe - ra - te
a - do - ra - re, qui - a ip - se est re - demp - ti - o mun - di.
Magi
Sal - ve Rex sae - cu - lo - rum! sus - ci - pe, Rex! au -
rum, tol - le thus, tu ve - re De - us, mirr - ham si - gnum se - pul -
Angelus
tu - rae! Im - ple - ta sunt om - ni - a, quae pro - phe - ti - ce dic - ta sunt,
ne vi - am re - me - an - tes a - li - am ne de - la - to - res

Magi
tan - ti re - gis pu - ni - en - di e - ri - tis. O re - gem coe - li.
Chorus
Internuntius
Te de - um lau - da - mus. De - lu - sus es do - mi - ne,
Armiger
Ma - gi vi - am re - di - e - runt a - li - am. De - cer - ne
do - mi - ne vin - di - ca - re i - ram tu - am, et stric - to mu -
cro - ne que - re - re ju - be pu - e - rum, for - te in - ter
Rex
oc - ci - sos oc - ci - de - tur et pu - er. In - cen - di - um me -
um ru - i - na e - o - rum ex - tin - guam in - do - lis
e - xi - mi - e pu - e - ros fac en - se pe - ri - re.

Prophetae Venientes Admonent

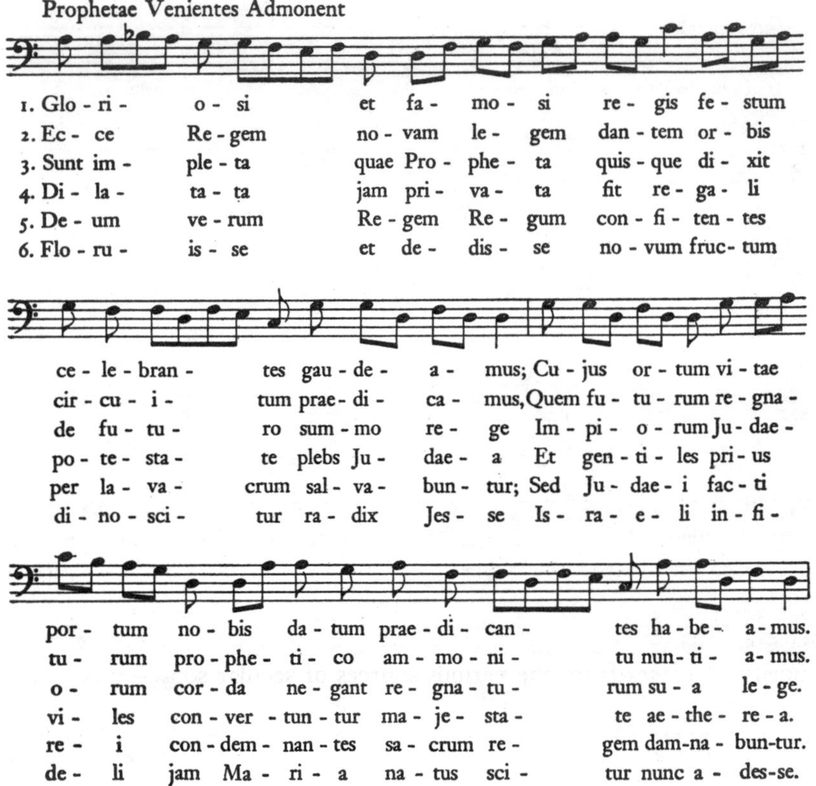
1. Glo - ri - o - si et fa - mo - si re - gis fe - stum
2. Ec - ce Re - gem no - vam le - gem dan - tem or - bis
3. Sunt im - ple - ta quae Pro - phe - ta quis - que di - xit
4. Di - la - ta - ta jam pri - va - ta fit re - ga - li
5. De - um ve - rum Re - gem Re - gum con - fi - ten - tes
6. Flo - ru - is - se et de - dis - se no - vum fruc - tum
ce - le - bran - tes gau - de - a - mus; Cu - jus or - tum vi - tae
cir - cu - i - tum prae - di - ca - mus, Quem fu - tu - rum re - gna -
de fu - tu - ro sum - mo re - ge Im - pi - o - rum Ju - dae -
po - te - sta - te plebs Ju - dae - a Et gen - ti - les pri - us
per la - va - crum sal - va - bun - tur; Sed Ju - dae - i fac - ti
di - no - sci - tur ra - dix Jes - se Is - ra - e - li in - fi -
por - tum no - bis da - tum prae - di - can - tes ha - be - a - mus.
tu - rum pro - phe - ti - co am - mo - ni - tu nun - ti - a - mus.
o - rum cor - da ne - gant re - gna - tu - rum su - a le - ge.
vi - les con - ver - tun - tur ma - je - sta - te ae - the - re - a.
re - i con - dem - nan - tes sa - crum re - gem dam - na - bun - tur.
de - li jam Ma - ri - a na - tus sci - tur nunc a - des - se.

Chorus

The Chorus repeats the first verse of the Prophets' Hymn *Glorioso et famosi* after each verse sung by the Prophets.

# 6. Bernart de Ventadorn
# Troubadour Canso, *Be m'an perdut*

This example and the two pieces that follow are songs characteristic of the large monophonic secular repertory that has come down to us from the twelfth and thirteenth centuries. The word "secular" is used in this connection broadly to include those songs of a religious but nonliturgical nature which arose outside the church and the abbey, such as the Spanish *cantiga* and the Italian *lauda* (Examples 7 and 8). Other types included in this repertory are the Latin monophonic *conductus*, Goliard songs, German Minnesinger melodies, and English songs; but the great majority of pieces from the various sources of secular song are troubadour and trouvère chansons: over 1600 melodies and more than 7500 poems are extant.

Secular medieval song first flowered in the twelfth century among the troubadours of Provence in Southern France, who wrote in the *langue d'oc*, or Provençal, a language still spoken today in that part of France. The origins of this secular song, whose texts mainly deal with the theme of courtly love, are not clear; the Crusades, Arabian influence, Gregorian chant, and popular song have all been held responsible to some degree for its rise. Whatever its origins, the Provençal movement spread over much of Western Europe, and the influence of the troubadours on secular lyrical song was profound and long-lasting; indeed, it may be said that it has never really died out, for many of the forms employed by the troubadours have remained in use ever since.

The troubadours expressed themselves in several well-defined poetic genres, chief of which was the *canso* (*canzone* or *chanson*), illustrated in this example. The canso was a particular musical form (described below), and the favored poetic vehicle for the expression of chivalric love. Some other poetic forms which dealt with special aspects of love were the *joc partit*, *alba*, and *pastorela;* the troubadours also wrote songs about moral and political questions (*sirventes*), satire (*eneug*), and mourning (*planh*).

The composer of Example 6 confined himself exclusively to love in the eighteen songs by him that have come down to us; unlike his fellow troubadours, he seems to have been indifferent to questions of politics, morality, and religion. Born in humble circumstances, Bernart nevertheless became a model for the *chantres de l'amour;* he must have contributed to the spread of troubadour art in the North, for he spent some time in Normandy at the court of his patroness, Eleanor of Aquitaine.

The songs of the troubadours are set strophically; that is, each verse of the poem is sung to the same melody. The musical form of the canso is that of a melodic segment which is repeated, and then followed by a third segment with fresh melodic material. *Be m'an perdut* follows this pattern. The first segment (measures 1–6) consists of two phrases; these are repeated (measures 6–12); the third segment (measures 13 to end) consists of three phrases, the last of which is a return to the melody of the second half of the first segment. Thus the outline is *a b, a b, c d b;* or, in broader terms, *A, A, B* (*A* in the second scheme represents both *a* and *b* of the first, and *B* of the second scheme is equivalent to *c, d,* and *b* of the first). This form is found in much of the secular music of the Middle Ages; it is very common in the melodies of the Minnesinger, where it is called the *Barform.* It is used in the *Meistergesang* of Hans Sachs (Example 22 in this book). When the last segment returns at the end to a phrase from the first segment, as in this example, the form is sometimes referred to as the *rounded chanson.* This is the form of the trouvère *ballade* and the fourteenth-century Italian madrigal. (See also Example 17.)

This piece, like many troubadour-trouvère songs, has a *tornada* or *envoi:* a concluding stanza addressed to the person for whom the song is written. The tornada of Example 6 is shorter than the other stanzas, and uses only the last part of the melody (measures 13–21). The phrasing of the melody is irregular because of the alternation of masculine and feminine endings in the successive lines of each stanza (except between lines five and six), and it is this irregularity which necessitates the insertion of an occasional half-measure when the piece is put in 6/4 meter.

The poem, *Be m'an perdut*, was also set to another, entirely different melody, perhaps by Bernart himself; the other version is printed in *HAM*, No. 18b.

The translation of the text:

1. I am indeed lost from the region of Ventadorn
To all my friends, for my lady loves me not;
With reason I turn not back again,
For she is bitter and ill-disposed toward me.
See why she turns a dark and angry countenance to me:
Because I take joy and pleasure in loving her!
Nor has she aught else with which to charge me.

2. So, like the fish who rushes to the lure
And suspects nothing until caught upon the hook,
Once I rushed to the overpowering love
And was not aware until I was in the flame
That burns hotter than ever furnace did.
And yet I cannot free my hands from it,
So greatly does my love hold and chain me.

3. I marvel not that love holds me fast,
For a more entrancing form, I believe, was never seen;
Beautiful and white she is, and fresh and smooth,
And wholly as I wish and desire her.
I can say no ill of her, for there is none in her;
Yet gladly would I say it if I knew any,
But I know none, and so forbear to speak it.

4. Ever shall I wish her honor and good,
And shall be her aid, her friend and servant,
And shall love her whether it please her or not,
For one cannot gainsay one's heart without destroying it.
I know no lady, whether she will or not,
Whom I could not love if I wished.
They all can bring one to grief, though.

5. To others, then, I am in forfeit;
Whichever will can draw me to her
On condition that what honor and benefit
She thinks to do me will not be sold too dearly,
For the seeking is grievous if sought in vain.
From experience I speak, for I have suffered,
And beauty has betrayed me badly.

6. To Provence I send joy and greeting
And more of good than I could speak.
And it is a wonder that I do this;
For I send that which I have not;
I have no joy save what is brought me

By my beauteous vision, and Sire Enchantment, my confident,
And Sire Pleasure, the Lord of Beaucaire.[1]

*Tornada*

My beauteous vision, God works such wonder through you
That no one seeing you would not be enraptured
Who knew what to tell you and what to do.

Source: C. Appel, *Bernart von Ventadorn*, Halle, 1915. Plate IX of this volume is a facsimile of the canso *Be m'an perdut* as it appears in a Milan manuscript known as Chansonnier G, fol. 14. Plate X shows a facsimile of the other melody to which this poem was set, and to which reference is made in the commentary. A modal transcription of Plate X is given in F. Gennrich, *Troubadours, Trouvères, Minne- und Meistersgesang*, Cologne, 1951.

[1] We do not know whether Bernart is referring to actual persons in these lines, or is using proper names metaphorically.

## 6. Bernart de Ventadorn (d. 1195)

## Troubadour Canso, *Be m'an perdut*

1. Be m'an per - dut lai en - ves Ven - ta - dorn tuih
2. Ais - si c·ol peis qui s'es - laiss' el ca - dorn e
3. No·m me - ra - vilh si s'a - mors me te pres, que
4. Totz tems vol - rai sa o - nor e sos bes e·lh
5. A las au - tras su - i (. . . .) es - cha - zutz; la
6. En Pro - en - sa tra - met jois e sa - lutz e
5
mei a - mic, pois ma dom - na no m'a - ma; et
no·n sap mot, tro que s'es pres en l'a - ma, m'es -
gen - ser cors no crei qu'el mon se mi - re: bels
se - rai om et a - mics e ser - vi - re, e
cals se vol, me pot vas se a - trai - re, per
mais de bes c'om no lor sap re - trai - re; e
es be dreihz que ja - mais lai no torn, c'a -
lais - sei eu vas trop a - mar un jorn, c'anc
e blancs es, e frescs e gais e les e
l'a - ma - rai, be li plass' o be·lh pes, c'om
tal co - ve que no·m si - a ven - dutz l'o -
fatz es - fortz, mi - ra - cles e ver - tutz, car

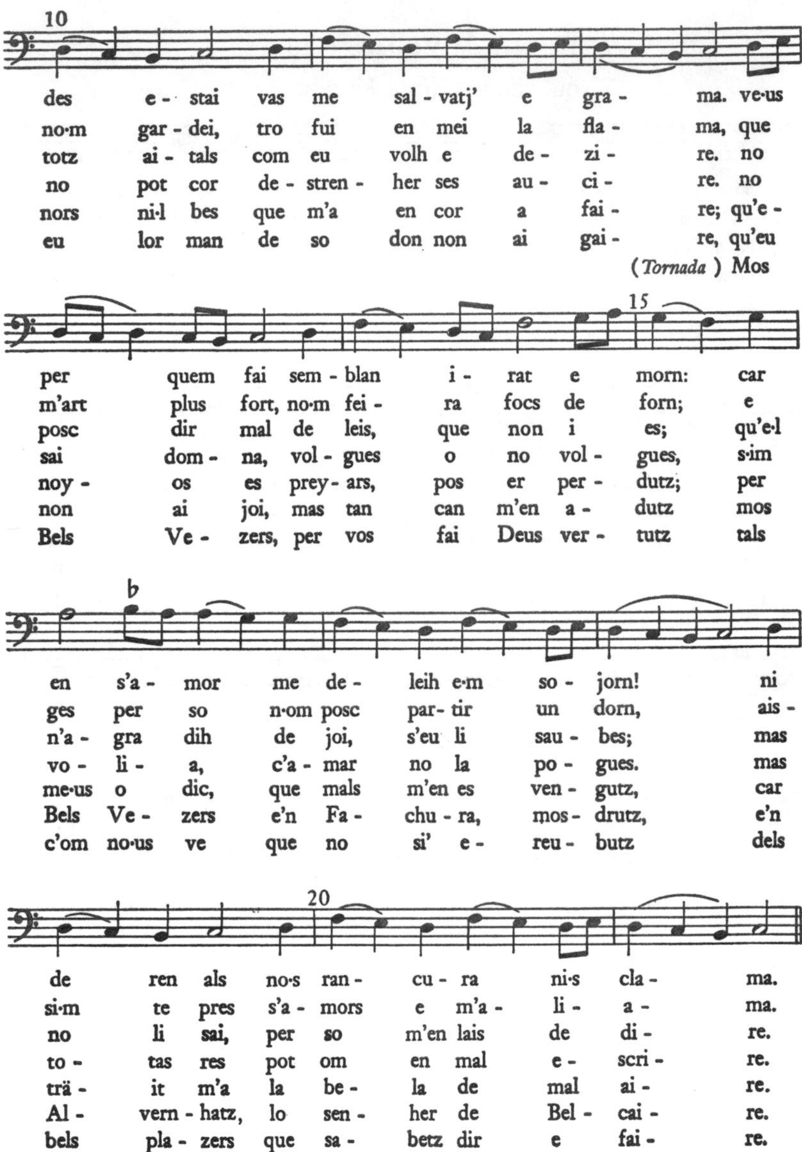
10
des e - stai vas me sal - vatj' e gra - ma. ve·us
no·m gar - dei, tro fui en mei la fla - ma, que
totz ai - tals com eu volh e de - zi - re. no
no pot cor de - stren - her ses au - ci - re. no
nors ni·l bes que m'a en cor a fai - re; qu'e -
eu lor man de so don non ai gai - re, qu'eu
(Tornada) Mos
15
per quem fai sem - blan i - rat e morn: car
m'art plus fort, no·m fei - ra focs de forn; e
posc dir mal de leis, que non i es; qu'e·l
sai dom - na, vol - gues o no vol - gues, s·im
noy - os es prey - ars, pos er per - dutz; per
non ai joi, mas tan can m'en a - dutz mos
Bels Ve - zers, per vos fai Deus ver - tutz tals
en s'a - mor me de - leih e·m so - jorn! ni
ges per so n·om posc par - tir un dorn, ais -
n'a - gra dih de joi, s'eu li sau - bes; mas
vo - li - a, c'a - mar no la po - gues. mas
me·us o dic, que mals m'en es ven - gutz, car
Bels Ve - zers e'n Fa - chu - ra, mos - drutz, e'n
c'om no·us ve que no si' e - reu - butz dels
20
de ren als no·s ran - cu - ra ni·s cla - ma.
si·m te pres s'a - mors e m'a - li - a - ma.
no li sai, per so m'en lais de di - re.
to - tas res pot om en mal e - scri - re.
trä - it m'a la be - la de mal ai - re.
Al - vern - hatz, lo sen - her de Bel - cai - re.
bels pla - zers que sa - betz dir e fai - re.

# 7. Alfonso El Sabio
## Cantiga, *Gran Dereit'*

---

The second of these three examples of medieval secular monophony comes from Galicia in Northwestern Spain, where the shrine of Santiago de Compostella, built over the supposed tomb of the apostle James, had from the ninth century been one of the chief places of pilgrimage in all Christendom. Among the many pilgrims in the twelfth and thirteenth centuries were troubadours and jongleurs from Provence, whose influence may have been partly responsible for the native Galician poetry. Much of this poetry was inspired by the worship of the Virgin Mary and her wonder-working powers. Of the many songs written to her, more than 400 were compiled by Alfonso X (1221–1284), King of Castile and Leon, who was called *El Sabio* ("the Wise") because of his love of art and science. Alfonso himself is thought to have composed the greater number of these songs, which exist in four manuscripts known collectively as *Las Cantigas de Santa Maria.*

In the Cantigas, over 350 miracles of the Virgin are told in the Galician dialect, which is akin to Portuguese; many of the miracles also appear in several other contemporary collections, such as the notable one of the monk-trouvère, Gautier de Coinci, *Les Miracles de la Sainte Vierge. Gran dereit'*, Example 7, is a characteristic and wholly charming story, the outline of which is contained in the heading (a practice common to all the cantigas), which, translated, reads: "This is how Saint Mary made five roses grow from the mouth of a monk after his death, because he had dedicated to her five psalms, each of which began with one of the five letters in her name." [1] The miracle is described in the six stanzas of the poem (translated below); the fourth stanza lists the psalms whose

[1] Esta é de como Santa María fez nacer as cinco rosas na boca do monge de pos sa morte, polos cinco salmos que dizía a onrra das cinco léteras que á no seu nome.

initial letters form the name *Maria,* although not in exact order. All the incipits refer to actual psalms except the *Magnificat,* the Virgin's song of thankfulness at the Annunciation.

The musical design of most of the cantigas is similar to that of the lauda (Example 8), and is probably a result of French influence, since it is essentially the design of the *virelai;* it consists of a refrain (called *estribillo*) at the beginning, which is also sung at the end of each verse (*estrofa*). In this cantiga the melodic plan of the refrain by phrases is *a b, a b′*, and that of the verse *c c′, c c′, a″ b, a b′;* the over-all plan of both refrain and verse is *A, B, A.* In actual performance it is likely that the singer may have felt free to sing the refrain only at the beginning and end, rather than after each of the several verses.

Certain of the cantigas, including this one, are written in a mensural ("measured") notation which indicates the rhythm clearly and definitely. The piece is in the (transposed) Ionian mode, and its rhythm is unmistakably Spanish in character. Spanish rhythm occurs in many of the other cantigas as well.

The translation:

*Estribillo*

A great delight it is,
This very beautiful miracle
Of the Virgin, through whom
Glorious God willed to be born for us.

*Estrofas*

Therefore I should like to recall
A miracle of which I heard,
And which you will enjoy
Hearing, and also
That you may know
Of the great good, as I learned,
That the Virgin had done
For a good monk.

He little knew how
To read, as I have heard,
But he knew how to adore
The Virgin, who has no peer.
And so he took
Five psalms and joined them,
For he believed in praising her,
And desired to do it thus.

Five psalms he chose,
And put them together
To make one of them all
For the five letters which are
In *Maria,* that he might take
Of her this reward:
That he should see
Her Holy Son.

He who sees and turns around
These psalms will find
*Magnificat* lying there,
And *Ad dominum;*
And at the end *In conver-
tendo* and *Ad te* will be,
And then *Retribue ser-
vo tuo,* most humbly.

To have God's favor, then,
Unfailingly each day
He went to say these psalms,
Prostrate before the altar,
And would repent
Of all that he feared
He might deserve
When he had been foolish and wretched.

This custom he maintained
While living in this world.
But after he had died
In his mouth appeared
A rosebush on which were seen
Five roses growing, and it grew
That it might bless
The mother of the Almighty One.

Source: El Escorial, T.j.I, fol. 32.

Modern edition: H. Anglès, ed., *La música de las Cantigas de Santa María del Rey Alfonso el Sabio,* II, Cantiga LVI, p. 64. Barcelona, 1943. A. Solalinde, ed., *Antología de Alfonso X el Sabio,* p. 23, Buenos Aires, 1941. Text only.

## 7. Alfonso El Sabio, Cantiga, *Gran dereit'*

Gran de - reit' é de se - er seu mi - ra - gre mui fre - mo - so
da Vir - gen, de que na - cer quís por nos Deus gro - ri - o - so.
1. Por en que - ro re - tra - er un mi - ra - gre que o - í,
2. Es - te sa - bí - a le - er pou - co, com' - o - i con - tar,
3. Dos sal - mos foi es - col - ler cin - que por es - ta ra - zón
4. Quen ca - tar' - et re - vol - ver es - tes sal - mos, a - cha - rá
5. Pe - ra ben de Deus a - ver. On - d'a - ques - tes, sen fa - lir,
6. Es - t'u - so foi man - tê - er men - tre no mun - do vi - veu;
on - d'a - ve - re - des pra - zer o - yn - do - o, ou - tro - sí
mas sa - bí - a ben que - rer a Vir - gen que non a par;
et des u - un os põ - er: por cin - que le - tras que son
*Ma - gni - fi - cat* y ia - zer et *Ad do - mi - num* y á,
sal - mos sem - pr'y - a di - zer ca - da dí - a sen men - tir
mas pois quand ouv' a mor - rer, na bo - ca ll'a - pa - re - ceu
per que po - de - des sa - ber o gran ben, com' a - pren - dí,
et por - en foi com - põ - er cin - que sal - mos et iun - tar,
en *Ma - rí - a* por pren - der d'e - la, poís, tal ga - lar - don,
et ca - bo d'el *In con - ver - ten - do* et *Ad te* es - tá,
an - t'o al - tar et ten - der - se to - do et re - pen - tir
ro - sal que ui - ron tê - er cin - que ro - sas, et cre - ceu
que a Vir - gen foi fa - zer a un bon re - li - gi - o - so.
por en sa lo - or cre - er, de que e - ra de - sei - o - so.
per que po - de - se ve - er o seu Fil - lo pi - a - do - so.
et pos *Re - tri - bu - e ser - vo tu - o* muit' - o - mil - do - so.
do que fo - ra me - re - cer quan - d'e - ra fol e as - tro - so.
por - que fo - ra bê - ei - zer Ma - dre do Po - de - ro - so.

# 8. Lauda
## *Ogne Homo*

Example 7 represents a type of religious song that appeared in the popular religious revivals which swept over Europe in the middle of the thirteenth century. Inspired by the example set by St. Francis of Assisi of joyfully embracing poverty, and also moved to penitence by the harrowing ills of the age, bands of penitents roamed in pilgrimage over the north of Italy, often practicing self-flagellation. It was in such a milieu that the popular songs of praise called *laude spirituali* arose, many of which have come down to us in manuscripts of the late thirteenth and early fourteenth centuries. With the encouragement of St. Francis, the "troubadour of religion," these songs were written in the vernacular. Francis himself is thought to be the author of some of the *laude* texts; his celebrated *Canticle of the Sun* is one of these texts, but the music to which it was set has been lost.

The lauda is of the greatest significance both because it was the first recorded awakening of the hitherto latent native Italian lyricism, and also because of its subsequent history. In the early fourteenth century a confraternity called the *Laudisti*, formed for the propagation of popular religious devotional singing, furthered the cultivation of this genre, which later came to be written in a simple homophonic style. A special type of semidramatic lauda in dialogue presented in the *oratorio* ("oratory," a place of prayer) of St. Philip Neri at Rome in the sixteenth century led to the rise of the oratorio, of which the earliest extant example is Cavalieri's *La Rappresentatione di anima e di corpo* (1600); see Example 37 of this book.

The lauda *Ogne homo* is from a collection of 123 pieces contained in two sumptuous manuscripts of the fourteenth century. Its notation uses single notes for the vowels which are syllabically set; those vowels which are set to groups of notes are written in ligature (literally, they are "tied" together), and each of these note-groups, whether of two, three, or four notes, is considered equal in value to a note standing alone. The natural phrasing of the piece so transcribed results in duple meter, and this is also true for most of the *laude* in the collection. Duple meter is a noteworthy feature of the lauda, for most of the monophonic music of the period when these songs were probably written is in triple meter. The use of duple meter suggests the popular origin of the *laude*, and reflects their national character; for Italian music, when compared with contemporaneous French music, displayed a marked predilection for duple meter.

The form of the piece is typical of most *laude:* a *ripresa* ("retaking," *i.e.*, refrain) of two two-measure phrases—up to the double bar; followed by a stanza comprised of two *piedi* ("feet") of two measures each; and a *volta* ("turn") of two further two-measure phrases in which the melody "turns" back to the melody of the refrain. In this lauda only the last measure is identical with the refrain, although the volta as a whole bears a distinct kinship to the ripresa; in other *laude* there are varying degrees of similarity between volta and ripresa. The refrain is sung after each stanza, so that the form as a whole is similar to the secular ballata; some of the other *laude* have a great many stanzas. Melodic rhyme occurs at the end of the three sections of ripresa, piede, and volta. The melody is in the Hypoaeolian mode, and its range is somewhat greater than that of most music of the period.

The text, translated:

Let every man raise high his voice
In praise of the true cross.

How worthy it is of praise
No heart can conceive,
No tongue can tell—
The true and holy cross.

This tree is precious
And a sign of virtue;
Our enemy is confounded
By the Death on the cross.

Source: Biblioteca Nazionale Centrale of Florence, Ms. Magliabechiano II, I, 122, fols. 25 and 25[v].

Modern edition: F. Liuzzi: *La lauda e i primordi della melodia italiana*, Vol. II, p. 68 (facsimile) and 69 (transcription), 1935. The author's transcription differs in some slight details from Liuzzi's.

## 8. Lauda (13th–14th century)

### *Ogne homo*

1.3.5. Og - ne ho - mo ad al - ta vo - ce
lau - di la ve - ra - ce cro - ce.
2. Quant' è de - gno
4. Ques - to è len - gno
da lau - da - re co - re nol - lo può pen - sa - re,
pre - ti - o - so et seg - no vir - tu - o - so,
lin - gua nol - lo può con - ta - re,
lo ne - mi - co è con - fu - so
la ve - ra - ce san - cta cro - ce.
per la mor - te de la cro - ce.

# 9. Leonin
# Organum Duplum, *Viderunt Omnes*

Examples 9 through 12 illustrate various phases of medieval polyphony of the twelfth and thirteenth centuries. Each of them is based in one way or another upon a Gregorian cantus firmus; they are in two, three, and four voice-parts; and they are characteristic products of the medieval technique of polyphonic composition by successive "layers" of melodic lines.

*Viderunt omnes*, Example 9, is a typical organum of the style known as *organum duplum* (that is, organum in two parts). Organum duplum, according to the theorists of the thirteenth century, had a somewhat special rhythmical character; however, they described the nature of this special character unsatisfactorily and ambiguously, and consequently modern scholars have interpreted the rhythm in various ways when transcribing organa dupla.

*Viderunt*, which was probably written by Leonin in the middle or late twelfth century, is musically halfway between the melismatic organum style which originated at the Abbey of St. Martial of Limoges in the early twelfth century (see the *Benedicamus Domino, M of M*, No. 8) and the organum triplum style of the so-called Notre Dame school of Paris in the late twelfth century (see the *Alleluya* of Perotin, *M of M*, No. 9). Like both of these pieces, *Viderunt* has a tenor consisting of a plainchant segment in which each note is treated as a sustained note of seeming (though not actual) indefinite length; like the second example, and unlike the first, it also has a section (measures 23–28) called a *clausula*, in which the notes of the tenor become shorter, and are measured in uniform time-values.

The notes of the tenor which are measured and thus form a clausula are not selected arbitrarily by the composer, but are notes used as a melisma in the original chant: for example, the "om-" of "omnes." The note, or small group of two or three notes, set to a single text syllable, are used for the long, sustained "pedal-points" of the organum. (See the quotation of the chant segment at the end of this commentary.)

Organum triplum has, in its two upper parts, composed melodies which are similar in melodic and rhythmic character; their rhythmic patterns are definite and clear, and are based on the rhythmic modes which supply the common rhythmical basis essential to their simultaneous performance. In organum duplum a common rhythmical factor is not essential except in the clausula. The notation in the earliest manuscript in which *Viderunt* appears shows that modal rhythm occurs in this passage and also in two other passages (measures 10–13 and 16–19), even though the tenor is not measured in these passages. Aside from these places, the rest of the duplum is notated in a manner that does not suggest any particular rhythmical character. The interpretation of these parts of the duplum by present-day scholars has ranged from a free rhythm like plainsong—the manner in which the St. Martial organa are assumed to have been sung—to a modally-measured delivery throughout.[1] *Viderunt* has been transcribed in Example 9 after a theory called the "consonance principle," which has been deduced by Willi Apel from certain passages in some thirteenth-century treatises. According to this principle, each of the upper notes consonant with the tenor is long (the consonances being the unison, octave, 5th, 4th, and 3rd), and each dissonant note is short. (See Apel, *JAMS*, Fall, 1949, p. 145, for a fuller explanation of the principle.)

Organum duplum is of the greatest historical significance. It is the oldest style of the polyphonic music which emerged at Paris and dominated Western music during the thirteenth century, and in it modal rhythm appears for the first time. The clausula sections, one or more of which appear in almost every organum, later developed into the most important polyphonic form of the Middle Ages, the *motet;* the motet came into being when these clausula sections were detached and ex-

[1] A facsimile reproduction of this organum from the famous Wolfenbüttel 677 ($W^1$) may be seen in *NMM*, Plate XXVIb. This will clarify the differences of notation found in the manuscript which are referred to above. Although $W^1$ was written down in the early fourteenth century, it contains pieces composed a long time before that, which are in a notation of a much earlier period.

panded, and words (*mots*) were added to the upper part, which was then called the *motetus*.

The tenor cantus firmus of *Viderunt omnes* ("They all saw") is the opening phrase of the Gradual for the Mass of the Day of the Nativity, and is given below. (See *LU*, p. 409.)

Source: Wolfenbüttel 677, fol. 21. Facsimile edition of this manuscript is J. Baxter, *An Early St. Andrews Music Manuscript*, London, 1931.

Modern editions: W. Apel, "From St. Martial to Notre Dame," *JAMS*, Fall, 1949, p. 145. W. Waite, *The Rhythm of Twelfth-Century Polyphony*, New Haven, 1954. "The Transcription," p. 67.

## 9. Leonin (12th century)

### Organum Duplum, *Viderunt omnes*

25
om -
30
35
nes.

# 10. Motet

## *Ave Gloriosa Mater—Ave Virgo—Domino*

---

The position of the motet in the music of the thirteenth and fourteenth centuries is not unlike that of the fugue in the Baroque era. The motet was a style, a manner of expression rather than a form; it could be sacred or secular, vocal or instrumental, and its basic design allowed for a great number of variations, which were thoroughly exploited by the Gothic constructive spirit. It has already been mentioned that the motet had its origin in the clausula of the organum; words were applied to the upper part of a two-voiced clausula, and the upper part was then called the *motetus* (which was also the name given to the entire composition) instead of the duplum. When a third voice was added above the duplum, it was called the *triplum*. Originally the motet was simply a polyphonic trope of the chant—more specifically, of that melisma of the chant which formed its tenor. Two different texts were used for the two upper parts, both of which paraphrased the idea of the cantus firmus. The musical texture of the motet was that of two upper voices of similar character, range, and rhythmical movement above a slower-moving plainchant tenor melody upon which a simple rhythmical figure was imposed.

The above description applies to the motet style of the first half of the thirteenth century (illustrated in *M of M*, No. 10); after that period it came to be modified in all sorts of ways without ever completely losing its original and essential musical character. Two important ways in which the motet of the second half of the thirteenth century came to differ from the earlier motet style are illustrated in *Ave gloriosa mater*. The first of these differences is the freer treatment of the cantus firmus. The tenor of this motet, for example, comes from the salutation *Benedicamus Domino* for the First Vespers of solemn feasts. The tenor incipit indicates that only the *Domino* section of the chant is used, but the melody is not literally quoted, as a comparison with the original chant will reveal. (See the quotation of the chant at the end of this commentary.) Instead, a more or less modified version of the original melody is used; the original melody is put into a repeated rhythmic pattern (*ordo*), in this example, a pattern of three notes. Halfway through the piece (beginning at measure 33) the tenor melody is repeated, this time with still further variation: a five-note rather than a three-note ordo is used. In general the extra two notes are treated in the manner of passing tones, and are usually inserted upon weak beats which do not occur in the original pattern. The general outline of the simpler version of the chant melody in measures 1–32 is followed, although it is departed from in several measures.

The other and more striking way in which this piece differs from the earlier motet style lies in the definite difference in the musical character of the motetus and the triplum. The motetus is in the first rhythmic mode (alternating long and short notes), with occasional slight rhythmic variations; the triplum proceeds in a movement of uniformly short notes (sixth mode), also varied from time to time. Thus the first half of the piece moves at three different rhythmical levels; in the second half the tenor takes on the same movement as the motetus.

The translation of the text:

*Triplum*

Hail, royal Virgin, mother of mercy,
Hail, thou full of grace, queen of glory,
Surpassing mother of an exalted offspring
Who sittest in the glory of the heavenly country,
In the court of the true King. Mother and daughter,
Abode of virtue and guiding star, on the throne of
Justice stay; let all the army of the heavenly host
Run to meet you, and to you let their harmonious
And manifold songs go before them.

Thou with such power, such victory,
With such surpassing beauty; mother and daughter,
Light of cleanliness and holy mother.
The celestial beings obey thee, the glowing objects of heaven
Are lost in wonder at the sight of thee, sun and moon and
All of heaven's stars.
O Virgin ruling on high, the angels above the firmament praise thee.
Hail, thou sure defence of the clergy, and true protection of the poor.

Thou art the pure improver of malice and the bearer of grace.
The gentle refuge of sinners, the consoling comfort of the sick.
Attend us after our death!
After the quick passing of this worthless generation,
Through grace, not through merit,
May thou lead us to the Father and to the Son.

*Motetus*

Hail, glorious mother of the Saviour,
Hail, beautiful Virgin, flower of chastity,
Hail, happy light, bride of splendor,
Hail, precious deliverance of sinners,
Hail, way of life, chaste, comely, pure,
Sweet, gentle, faithful, happy creature.
Mother in a marvelous way of a newly born,
Of a man, but without a man, contrary to the laws of man.
Virgin of virgins, without reproach,
Splendor that rules the light of heaven,
Health of the people, light of the faithful,
Light of hearts, enlighten us,
And with thy son so holy and so auspicious reunite us,
And to our eternal joys pray lead us,
O holy virgin Mary.

The segment of the plainchant *Benedicamus Domino* from which the tenor cantus firmus of Example 10 is derived (see *LU*, p. 124):

Source: Bamberg, Staatsbibliothek, Ed. IV 6, fol. 1.

Modern edition: P. Aubry: *Cent motets du XIII[e] Siècle*, Paris, 1908. This is an edition of the Bamberg Codex with facsimile reproduction of the entire manuscript in Vol. I, transcriptions in Vol. II, and commentary in Vol. III. Example 10 appears on fol. 1 of Vol. I, and is transcribed in Vol. II, p. 1.

## 10. Motet (13th century)

*Ave gloriosa mater–Ave Virgo–Domino*

A - ve, Vir - go re - gi - a, Ma- ter cle - men- ci - e, A - ve, ple -
A - ve glo - ri - o - - sa Ma - ter sal - va -
Domino
na gra - ci - a. Re - gi - na glo - ri - e, Ge - ne - trix e - gre - gri
to - - ris, A - ve, spe - ci - o - - sa
5
a Pro- lis ex - i - mi - ne, Que se - des in glo - ri - a Ce - les -
Vir - go, flos pu - do - ris, A - ve, lux io -
tis pa - tri - e, Re - gis ve - ri re - gi - a Ma - ter et fi - li -
co - - sa, Tha - la - mus splen - do - - ris,
10

a, Cas - trum pu - di - ci - ci - e Stel - la - que pre - vi - a,
A - ve pre - ci - o - - sa Sa - lus pec - ca -
In tro - no jus - ti - ci - e Re - si - de ob - vi - a Ag - mi - na
to - - ris. A - ve, vi - te vi - a,
mi - li - ci - e Ce - les - tis om - ni - a Oc - cur - runt mi - li - ci -
Cas - ta, mun - da, pu - ra Dul - cis, mi - tis,
e Que ti - bi pre - vi - a can - ti - ca sim - pho - ni - e Tam mul -
pu - - ra, Fe - lix cre - a - tu - ra,
ti - pha - ri - a. Tu tan - te po - ten - ci - e, Tan - te vic - to - ri -
Pa - rens mo - do mi - - ro No - va pa - ri -

e, For - me tam e - gre - gi - e Ma - ter et fi - li - a.
30
tu - ra, Vi - rum si - ne vi - - ro
Lux mun-di - ci - e Ge - ni - trix- que pi - a, O - be - di - unt ti - bi
Con - tra car - nis iu - ra. Vir - go vir - gi -
ce - les - ti - a, Ce - li lu - mi - na - ri - a Stu - pe - fi -
35
num, Ex - pers cri - mi - num,
unt de tu - a spe - ci - e Sol et lu - na cun - cta que po - lo -
De - cus lu - mi - num, Ce - li do - mi -
40
rum sy - de - ra. Vir - go re - gens su - pe - ra, Te lau- dant an -
na, Sa - lus gen - ci - um,

ge - li su - per e - the - ra. A - ve, cle - ri tu - tum pre - si - di -
45
Lux fi - de - li - um, Lu - men cor - di -
um Pau - pe - ris - que ve - rum sub - si - di - um, Tu es pu -
um, Nos il - lu - mi - na.
ra li - ma ma - li - ci - e Et al - la - trix gra - ci - e,
50
Nos - que fi - li - o Tu - o tam pi -
Pec - ca - to - rum mi - te re - fu - gi - um, E - gro - tan - ci - um So -
o Tam pro - pi - ci - o
la - bi - le so - la - ci - um, No - bis as - sis post o - bi - tum,
55
Re - con - ci - li - a, Et ad gau - di -

Post is- ti- us se-cu- li vi- te vi- lis tran si- tum,
a Nos per-hen- ni- a
Per gra-ci- am, non per me- ri- tum Du-cas nos ad
Duc pre-ce pi- a
Pa- trem et Fi- li- - - um.
Vir - go Ma- - ri- - a.

# 11. Instrumental Motet (Hocket)
## *In Seculum Longum*

The music that follows actually comprises two compositions (Example 11–12) which illustrate further the medieval technique of composing by layers of melodic lines. One aspect of this technique was seen in Example 10, in which a new triplum was substituted for an older one in a three-voiced motet. In Example 11–12 a three-voiced instrumental motet is changed into a four-voiced vocal motet by the addition of a quadruplum consisting of a new melody with a text. An essential feature of Example 11 is the use of *hocket* throughout in the two voices above the tenor (that is, the breaking up of a melody into single notes —or very small figures—which are performed in quick alternation by two performers). The name *hoketus* ("hocket") was used by contemporary theorists not only in reference to the hocket technique itself, but also to describe a piece in motet style in which hocketing is used persistently, as it is here.

The original three-voiced instrumental motet on which this piece is based is written on the two lower staves of Example 11–12; the tenor cantus firmus occupies the bottom staff, while the two upper parts are on the middle staff. The composition appears thus in the Bamberg Codex (late thirteenth century) as one of a set of five compositions without text that use the *In seculum* tenor. In the great Montpellier Codex of about the same period the same piece appears with the quadruplum *Je n'amerai autre* added, the three lower parts being identical with the Bamberg *In seculum longum* except for slight differences in the latter which are indicated by smaller notes placed between the staves.

The tenor cantus firmus is from the Gradual *Haec dies* of the Mass for Easter; the original phrase is given at the end of this commentary.

It has been rhythmicized with a simple three-note ordo, and comes to an end on the first beat of measure 23. On the second half of this measure the melody begins again. It is quoted literally as far as its pitch successions are concerned, but takes on a different character because the beginning of the ordo is now made to fall on a different note and thus no longer coincides with the beginning of the original melody. This device was frequently employed in the motets of the thirteenth and fourteenth centuries (an instance occurs in the tenor of *M of M*, No. 10).

Above the tenor, the motetus and triplum proceed in a movement dominated throughout most of the composition by hocket technique, in which one voice—usually the upper—plays a single note, followed immediately by the same note in the other voice, the two notes being put in the second rhythmic mode (alternating short and long values). Fleeting passages of brief imitation occur at measures 15–16 and 44–45; the first of these is brought about by an exchange of parts between the two voices (German, *Stimmtausch*). The harmony follows the thirteenth-century principle of employing perfect intervals and occasional thirds, major and minor, on strong beats; a second or a seventh appears infrequently in the manner of an appoggiatura.

The instrumental motet *In seculum longum* forms part of the small extant repertory of medieval instrumental music, which consists for the most part of dances of the *estampie* type. (See *M of M*, No. 12.) One of the five compositions in the Bamberg set that uses the *In seculum* tenor is the famous *In seculum viellatoris* ("The *In seculum* of the viol player"; see *GMB*, No. 20); this is the earliest reference in music to an actual instrument. The word "longum" in the title of Example 11 refers to the movement of the tenor, which is in the fifth rhythmic mode throughout, hence always proceeds in longs. Another composition in the set is entitled *In seculum breve*, and has the same notes in all its parts as *In seculum longum*, but is in an entirely different rhythm. (The latter piece is reproduced in facsimile from the Bamberg Codex in *NMM*, Plate XXXVI, and shows the same style of notation employed in Example 11.)

# 12. Vocal Motet
## *Je n'amerai autre—In Seculum*

Example 12 is the music on all three staves of Example 11–12; the upper staff bears the added quadruplum which has transformed the three-part instrumental hocket-motet *In seculum longum* into the four-part vocal motet *Je n'amerai autre.* (This same melody was also added to the *In seculum breve* referred to above, its rhythm being changed to accommodate the rhythm of that version.) The changes made in the instrumental parts are negligible; most of them consist simply of employing a single note of dotted-half value whenever two repeated notes of dotted-quarter value occur in the earlier version, as in measures 29, 35, 39, and 45.

The additional part is quite different in character from the music of the lower parts; it is smoothly flowing in rhythm and melody, and has varied rhythmic patterns in which there is a predominance of the second rhythmic mode (see commentary to Example 11). In a very few places the quadruplum proceeds in a hocket movement against the lower voices, as in measures 13–14 and 41–43, or shows slight imitation with them, as at measures 14–16 and 38–39. Sometimes it doubles a lower voice for a brief stretch, as at measures 25–26. It is treated in the same harmonic terms as the lower voices, but occasionally a striking dissonance is introduced. Whenever a dissonant note occurs, however, it will be observed that it is consonant with one of the other voices, a principle of thirteenth-century composition explained by contemporary theorists—for example, Franco of Cologne. (See *SR*, p. 155.)

The composition thus presents an unusual and interesting texture consisting of three different levels of melodic and rhythmical activity, including the steady motion of the tenor, the syncopated rhythms of the two inner parts, and the flowing movement of the vocal melody at the top. It is one of the earliest examples in the history of music in which the combination of voices and instruments is clearly indicated, even though the nature of the instruments used for the three lower voices can only be conjectured.

The question of the use of musica ficta (*i.e.*, accidentals that were understood, but not indicated) in this composition is a difficult one. The editor has been conservative in the addition of such indications, and has not attempted to make all diminished fifths perfect, as the practice of the thirteenth century appears to include the use of this interval in open chords without the third.

The translation of the text:

I shall have no other than her
Whom I have loved with a true heart;
I have given her my love,
Never shall I part from her,
Come snow or frost.

Lord! What shall I tell her, the beauty
Who has my heart and my love?
Because of her I am in great pain,
Nor have I rest by night or day
When I behold her little mouth,
Her very fresh complexion.

Her attire is not unhandsome,
My plaint is one of sweetness,
Of courtliness and honor.
Oh sweet friend, life is too long,
I am always in tears for you;
Lighten for me my great pain!

The *In seculum* tenor (see also *LU*, pp. 778–79):

Sources: Bamberg, Stiftsbibliothek, Ed. IV 6, fol. $63^v$. Montpellier, Fac. des Médecins H 196, fol. $1^v$.

Modern editions: P. Aubry: *Cent Motets du XIII$^e$ Siècle*, Paris, 1908. Example 11 appears on fol. $63^v$ of Vol. I; Aubry's transcription on p. 224 of Vol. II.

Y. Rokseth: *Polyphonies du XIII^e Siècle*, Paris, 1936–39. This is an edition of the Montpellier Codex with facsimile reproduction of the entire manuscript in Vol. I, transcriptions in Vols. II and III, Commentary in Vol. IV. Ex. 12 is on fol. 1^v of Vol. I; Rokseth's transcription on p. 2 of Vol. II. The author's transcription differs in some details from both Aubry's and Rokseth's.

11. Instrumental Motet (Hocket), *In seculum longum*

12. Vocal Motet, *Je n'amerai autre–In seculum*

Je n'a - me - rai au - tre que ce - le que j'ai de fin cuer a -
In seculum longum
5
mé - e; je li ai m'a - mour dou - né - e, ne ja
10
ne me par - ti - rai de li pour noif ne pour
15
ge - lé - e. Dieus, que li di - rai, la

be - le qui a mon cuer et m'a - mour? Pour li
20
sui en grant do - lour, n'i ai re - pos ne nuit ne
25
jour quant je re - mir sa bou - che - te, sa tres
30
fre - che - te cou - lour. Ses a - tours n'est

35
pas vi - lains, mes plains est de dou - çor, de cour - toi - sie
et d'ou - nour. Hé douce a - mi - e, trop
40
main du - re vi - e, en plour tous jours pour
45
vous sui; a - le - giés moi mes grans do - lours.

# 13. *Agnus Dei*
## From the Mass of Tournai

This is the first of a group of six compositions (Examples 13 through 18) which offer a cross-section of various styles and techniques of late medieval music. Each piece is a product, directly or indirectly, of a new musical style introduced in France in the fourteenth century, called the Ars Nova; each illustrates some phase of the expansion and elaboration of musical devices which arose in the early fourteenth century. In this century polyphonic settings of the Ordinary of the Mass began to appear; of these six pieces, three treat the music of the Mass in various ways—a straightforward setting of the *Agnus Dei* (Example 13), an elaborate trope of a *Kyrie* for voices and instruments (Example 14); and an early example of an Organ Mass (Example 15). Two pieces of secular vocal music—one French, the other Italian—follow; the last example is an isorhythmic motet.

Historically, the Tournai Mass is distinguished among all other compositions of this genre as being the earliest known polyphonic cycle of the Ordinary. Only five such works have come down to us from the fourteenth century, one of these being the celebrated Mass of Guillaume de Machaut (see *M of M*, No. 13). The Mass of Tournai, a town in that part of Western Belgium known as French Flanders (Flemish, *Doornik*), exists in a manuscript from the early part of the fourteenth century, and may be a collection of compositions written by more than one composer and at different periods, as there are stylistic differences in certain of the items.

The *Agnus* is set in a simple conductus style in which the voices proceed uniformly in a third-mode rhythm, with occasional independent movement at cadences, and with a trace of hocket in the second phrase (measures 8–10 and 11). It is syllabic except for the melismas on the "no-" of "nobis" in the second phrase, and the "pa-" of "pacem" in the last phrase. The character of the pieces is harmonically "firmer" than that of the music of the Ars Antiqua; in modern harmonic terms, it shows an expansion of thirteenth-century harmonic practice in its free use of the chord of the sixth (3-5-8) as well as of the open triad (1-5-8) on strong beats. The triad (1-3-5) also appears in this position, though less often than the other two chords.

The cadences are invariably of the type known as the "double leading tone" cadence: the penultimate chord is a sixth, from which the tenor moves downward a whole step, while the motetus and triplum each move upward a half step to the 5th and 8ve respectively: that is, the movement is that of a sixth chord expanding to an open triad. The designation "double leading tone" arises from the concept, in modern terms, that the middle voice in the penultimate chord is the raised-fourth degree of the scale; hence the cadence gives the effect of involving both tonic and dominant keys. This cadence is seen in simple form at the end of the second phrase, and in various ornamental forms at the ends of the other phrases.

Music like that of Example 13, although simple, is capable of creating a strong and definite mood; it owes its effect largely to its stark, somber harmony, which is not very far removed from many a passage in twentieth-century music.

The text:

O Lamb of God, that takest away the sins of the world,
have mercy upon us.
O Lamb of God, that takest away the sins of the world,
have mercy upon us.
O Lamb of God, that takest away the sins of the world,
grant us thy peace.

Source: Bibliothèque de l'Église Cathédrale de Tournai, Ms. Voisin IV, fol. 33.

Modern editions: C. van den Borren, *Missa tornacensis*, p. 31, 1957. L. Schrade, *Polyphonic Music of the Fourteenth Century*, Vol. I, p. 128, Monaco, 1956.

## 13. *Agnus Dei* (14th century)

### From the Mass of Tournai

mi - se - re - re no - - bis. A - gnus de - i, qui tol -
20
mi - se - re - re no - - bis. A - gnus de - i, qui tol -
mi - se - re - re no - bis. A - gnus de - i, qui tol -
lis pec - ca - ta mun - di: do - na no - bis pa -
25
lis pec - ca - ta mun - di: do - na no - bis pa -
lis pec - ca - ta mun - di: do - na no - bis pa -
- - - - - - - - - cem.
30
35
- - - - - - - - - cem.
- - - - - - - - - cem.

# 14. Fronciaco
# Trope of a Kyrie

In the period from the ninth through the fourteenth centuries many additions and interpolations were made to the fixed, authorized texts and melodies of the Roman liturgy. While these additions all come under the generic term of *tropes* (from the Latin *tropus*, "figure of speech," adapted from the Greek *tropos*, "turn"), the word itself is most often used in reference to the medieval practices of adding words to a melisma in a chant, and inserting new musical and verbal phrases into chants. Troping was important because it offered an outlet for free composition in the realm of sacred music, and even though tropes were officially banned from the liturgy by the Council of Trent, they opened the way for many important developments in creative music. Only the special form of trope known as the sequence (or *Alleluia* trope) remained in liturgical use, and only five of these are still sung, being reserved for certain special festivals. (See *M of M*, No. 3.)

Troping appears most frequently in the various parts of the Ordinary of the Mass (though rarely in the Credo), particularly in the Kyrie. An interesting vestige of the practice of troping survives in the names that are attached to several of the Masses in use today—*Kyrie fons bonitatis*, *Kyrie Deus sempiterne*, etc.; these names indicate the tropes that once were added to the melismas of the Kyries of these Masses. Text tropes had a function: they amplified or explained the meaning of the original text. Particularly striking manifestations are those tropes of the Epistles which are vernacular explanations of the Biblical text—the "*Épîtres farcies*."

The earliest tropes were monophonic like the chant itself, of course; but later tropes were composed in the style of writing that developed with the rise and growth of polyphony. Some of the polyphonic tropes, like Example 15, were quite highly organized compositions.

Example 15 is from a manuscript that contains pieces by several well-known French composers, such as Dufay, Vitry, and Tapissier; however, some of the composers represented in this manuscript are otherwise unknown, like Fronciaco, the composer of this example. His conception of the trope is original and imaginative, and combines several striking features. The literary part of the trope, a devotional meditation on the Saviour and His meaning for mankind, consists of a series of three stanzas that are interpolated between the two words in each of the liturgical invocations—*Kyrie* (trope) *eleison; Christe* (trope) *eleison; Kyrie* (trope) *eleison*—with rhyming words in the middle of each line as well as at the end. The melody to which the text is set is not in this case a preexistent chant, but was written by the composer. The tenor, the lowest part in the score, is a cantus firmus on the melodies of the first phrase in each of the three exclamations in the Kyrie of Mass IX. (The original Gregorian Kyrie is given at the end of this commentary.)

The counterpoint has the marked independence of individual lines that is typical of much Ars Nova writing. However, it will be noted that there is a kind of pairing of the two upper voices against the others; each pair is in marked contrast, which results in a musical texture characteristic of many of the four-part compositions of the epoch, for instance, the Agnus Dei of the Mass of Machaut (*M of M*, No. 13). There, as in the Kyrie Trope, the two voices at the bottom are similar in rhythmical and melodic character, and are pitted against two upper voices very much livelier in rhythmical pace and variety, and also similar to one another in musical character.

Following is the translation of the text:

*Trope*

| | | |
|---|---|---|
| Lord | Sweetest Jesus, true Father of piety,<br>Eternal King in the highest, source of all goodness,<br>Saviour most merciful, excelling power of brightness, | have mercy upon us. |
| Christ | Brightness and form of the Father, thou did'st take on our flesh,<br>Maker made creature, Thou did'st put on our flesh,<br>Thus the nature of both remains, God [and man?], | have mercy upon us. |

Lord { I hail Thee, I look after Thee, good Jesus, author of light:
I gaze upon Thee, I seek after [Thee], who by thy [light?] dost ever lead:
I strive after Thee, I sigh for Thee, rising over the wood of the cross: } have mercy upon us.

These are the phrases of the Kyrie chant, Mass IX (*Cum jubilo*), which form the tenor of Example 14 (see also *LU*, p. 40):

Ky - ri - e e - le - i - son.
Chri - ste e - le - i - son.
Ky - ri - e e - le - i - son.

Source: A manuscript in the library of the Cathedral of Apt.
Modern edition: A. Gastoué: *Le Manuscrit de Musique du Trésor d'Apt*, p. 33, Paris, 1936. The Kyrie trope (fol. $9^v$ of the manuscript), is reproduced in color facing p. 33. The author's transcription differs in several details from Gastoué's.

## 14. Fronciaco (14th century)

### Trope of a Kyrie

1. Ky - - - - ri - e, Jhe - su dul - cis - si -
2. Ky - - - - ri - e, e - ter - ne rex al - tis - si -
3. Ky - - - - ri - e, sal - va - tor cle - men - tis - si -
Triplum
Contratenor
Tenor
me, pa - ter ve - re pi - e - ta - tis, e - - -
me, fons to - ci - us bo - ni - ta - tis, e - - -
me, pre - sta re - gnum cla - ri - ta - tis, e - - -
- ley - son. 1. Chri - ste,
- ley - son. 2. Chri - ste,
- ley - son. 3. Chri - ste,

15
splen - dor pa - tris et fi - gu - ra,
fac - tor fac - tus cre - a - tu - ra,
sic u - tra - que stat na - tu - ra,
20
no - stram car - nem sus - ce - pi - sti, e - -
car - nem no - stram in - du - i - sti, e - -
cau - te De - us [________], e - -
25
(♩ = ♩.)
ley - - - - son. 1. Ky - - - - ri -
ley - - - - son. 2. Ky - - - - ri -
ley - - - - son. 3. Ky - - - - ri -
12
8

30
e, Te sa- lu-to, te re- qui-
e, Te in- tu-to [te] per- qui-
e, Te af- fec-to, te sus- pi-
35
ro, bo- ne Jhe- su, auc- tor lu- cis,
ro, qui tu- o [?] sem- per du- cis,
ro, pro- ce- dens [?] li- gnum cru- cis,
e- - - - ley- son.
e- - - - ley- son.
e- - - - ley- son.

# 15. Organ Paraphrase of a Kyrie

Until recent years the only known instrumental polyphonic music of the fourteenth century consisted of a few pages containing keyboard dances from the Robertsbridge Codex in the British Museum, and a keyboard version of a ballata by Francesco Landini in the Reina Codex of the Bibliothèque Nationale in Paris. (For facsimile illustrations of these see *NMM* Plates XL and XLI. The style of notation used in Plate XL is identical with that in which Example 15 was written.) To this meager store a large and valuable collection of over a hundred pages of instrumental compositions was added in 1939 with the discovery of the manuscript known as Codex Faenza 117. The instrumental pieces in this manuscript are for the most part transcriptions of a number of secular French and Italian compositions of the Ars Nova, including works by Guillaume de Machaut, Jacopo da Bologna, Bartolino da Padova, and Francesco Landini. One of the pieces is the paraphrase of a Gregorian Kyrie, Example 15.

The Kyrie, like the other instrumental music in the Faenza manuscript, is written in score notation—that is, the two voice parts of the piece are arranged on two adjacent staves; the notes of the lower voice are under those of the upper part with which they are intended to coincide, and bar lines are employed. The significance of the use of score notation is that it is an almost certain indication that the composition was intended for performance on a solo instrument capable of playing polyphonic music. This would be a keyboard instrument, either an organ, clavichord, or spinet; for this Kyrie it may be assumed that an organ of the type known as the positive was used.

The tenor of the example is the melody of the first invocation of the Kyrie of the Gregorian Mass No. IV (*Cunctipotens Genitor Deus*). A comparison of the tenor with the melody from the Mass (quoted at the end of this commentary) will reveal a slight degree of coloration (measures 12 and 17), and a slight modification of the last couple of notes before the final note; otherwise they are identical.

The figurations in the upper part display considerable invention, the device of the sequence being especially notable (measures 5–6, 20–21, and elsewhere). These figures, as well as scale passages, broken thirds, and repetition of rhythmic figures, are characteristic of a kind of idiomatic writing that did not appear again in music until the sixteenth century.

The intervals most frequently used when the two parts coincide at the beginning of each bar are the 8ve, 5th, and 3rd, with single instances each of the 6th, 7th, and unison.

The Kyrie paraphrase has the additional interest of being one of the earliest known examples of the organ Mass, a genre whose long history extends from the fourteenth to the early eighteenth century. In the organ Mass, which was usually confined to the Ordinary, sections of each Mass item were set polyphonically for the organ, and alternated with sections sung by the choir in plainchant. Thus, in the ninefold evocation of the Kyrie, the organ paraphrase of this example would be followed by the unison chant sung by the choir alone, after which the organ paraphrase would be repeated; the first and third Christe evocations would be in plainchant, the second set in an organ version; in the last three Kyrie evocations, the first and third would be played by the organ, the second sung by the choir. The other Mass items were treated similarly, although less regularly than the Kyrie because of the nature of their texts. An analogous example of this *alternatim* practice, as it was called, is seen in the *Magnificat* of Morales, Example 23 of this book, in which alternate verses of the *Magnificat* are set polyphonically, the verses between being intended for performance in plainchant.

The opening Kyrie invocation of Mass IV (see also *LU*, p. 25):

Source: Faenza, Biblioteca Communale 117, fol. 28.

Modern edition: D. Plamenac: "Keyboard Music of the 14th Century in Codex Faenza 117," *JAMS*, Fall, 1951, p. 192. A facsimile reproduction of the pages of the Faena Codex containing the Kyrie paraphrase faces page 192.

## 15. Organ paraphrase of a Kyrie (14th century)

20
25

# 16. Giovanni da Firenze
## Caccia, *Con brachi assai*

---

The *caccia* ("hunt," or "chase") is one of the three secular forms favored by Italian composers of the Trecento (fourteenth century), the other two being the *ballata* and the *madrigal* (see *M of M*, No. 14). Of the large number of compositions in these forms, only twenty *cacce* are extant, although in many ways the caccia is the most interesting style of composition from this period, both from a musical and literary standpoint. As the name implies, the subject of the caccia text is a hunting scene, with lively descriptions of the various incidents attached to the hunt, such as the calls of the hunters, and other realistic touches. By transference the name came to be used for other naturalistic descriptions, such as fishing, market scenes, and even a fire. The composer of *Con brachi assai*, Giovanni da Firenze (also known as Johannes de Florentia and Giovanni da Cascia) was one of the first of the rising and important school of Italian Ars Nova musicians; he was active about a generation before Francesco Landini, with whom he compares in musical invention and inspiration.

Unlike the other two secular Trecentist forms, the caccia had a particular musical texture consisting of two solo voices in strict canon at the unison (called "Primus" and "Secundus" in the manuscript from which Example 16 is taken) and an independent instrumental "Tenor" in longer note values which supplied a harmonic underpinning to the livelier upper parts. In most *cacce* there is a second section (*ritornello*) which is also written in canonic style, and usually in contrasting meter to the first section. The ritornello is not an indispensable feature of the caccia (some examples do not have one), nor is the canonic style essential to the ritornello.

The caccia *Con brachi assai* is characteristic of this genre. The text describes a bird hunt, during the course of which a sudden shower occurs. The reference to Dido and Aeneas in the ritornello draws an amorous, playful analogy between the rainstorm and the tempest which drove the Trojan hero Aeneas to the shores of Carthage, where he was so hospitably received by Queen Dido. In the Panciatichi Codex, from which this example comes, the text is set to two different musical versions; in each of these, another stanza, which parallels the stanza written to the music of the first section, is added after the end of the composition. This text has been arranged here under the text of the first stanza, and is to be sung immediately after that stanza and before the ritornello.

The caccia opens with a typical melisma on the first syllable; the variety of note values employed helps each of the two voices keep its identity when the canon begins, in spite of continual crossing. The flow of the melody is interrupted by the excited cries of the hunters; at these places hocket, a device common to nearly all *cacce*, is used effectively for animation (for example, measures 14 and 17).

An effective contrast is achieved in the ritornello by the change from duple to triple meter, and also by the closer entry of the canonizing voice; the change of musical character accords well with the change of scene and mood in the text. At no time in the caccia does the instrumental part share in the motivic interplay, although this is not true of all *cacce*. The instrumental part preserves a contrivedly neutral character, although it is not without melodic interest.

The text, translated:

With hounds aplenty and hawks galore
We hunted birds on Ad(d)a's shore;
Some cried: "Go to't!" and others "O'er here!"
"Varin!" "Come back, Picciolo!"
Still others took the quail right on the wing,
When a stormy downpour came.

Never did greyhounds run through the land
As did each hunter, to flee the storm;
Some cried: "Give't here! Give me the cloak!"
And thus: "Give me the hat!"—
When I took cover, with my bird,
Where a shepherdess struck me to the heart.

*Ritornello*

She was alone there, so to myself I said:
"Here's the rain! Here are Dido and Aeneas!"

Source: Florence, Biblioteca Nazionale Centrale, Panciatichi 26, fol. 93v.
Modern editions: N. Pirrotta: *The Music of Fourteenth Century Italy*, Vol. I, p. 44, Amsterdam, 1954. W. Marrocco: *Fourteenth-Century Italian Cacce*, p. 15, Cambridge, 1942. This edition contains both settings of *Con brachi assai*, p. 15 and p. 18.

## 16. Giovanni da Firenze (14th century)

### Caccia, *Con brachi assai*

ce - - va: "Da, da!" E,
ce - - a: "Da, qua!" "Dam -
15
per la ri va d'A- da; E qual di -
cun per fug gir l'ac - qua; E qual di -
E qual: "Va cià, Va - rin!
mi'l man tel - lo!" E tal:
ce - va: "Da, da!" E,
ce - a: "Da, qua!" "Dam -
Tor - na, Pic - cio - lo!" E
"Dam - mi'l cap - pel - lo!" Quan - - - - - - -
20
E qual: "Va cià, Va - rin!
mi'l man - tel - lo!" E tal:
- - - - - - - - - - -
Tor - na Pic- cio - lo!" E
"Dam - mi'l cap- pel - lo!" Quan - - - - - - - -
qual pren - de a le qua - glie a vo - lo a vo - lo,
- - - d'io ri - co - ve - rai co'l mio uc - cel - lo,
- - - - - - - - - - - - - - -

Quan -
Do -
25
qual pren - de a le
d'io ri - co - ve -
qua-glie a vo - lo a vo - lo, Quan -
rai co'l mio uc - cel - lo, Do -
do con gran tem - pe - sta u - n'ac - qua ven -
ve-u - na pa - stu - vel - la'l cor mi pun -
30
do con gran tem - pe - sta u n'ac - qua ven -
ve-u - na pa - stu - rel - la'l cor mi pun -
ne.
se.
ne.
se.
So - la e - ra li, on - de fra
35
So - la e - ra li, on -

me di - ce - a: “Ec - - co la piog - gia!
40
de fra me di - - ce - a: “Ec - -
Ec - co Di - do et E - -
co la piog - gia! Ec - co Di - do
ne - - - - - - - - - - a!”
45
et E - ne - - - - - - - - - a!”

# 17. Anthonello de Caserta
## Ballade, *Notes pour moi*

By the second half of the fourteenth century, many musicians were writing only secular music; many of the extant manuscripts of this period contain nothing else. Some of these codices, such as the one from which Example 16 comes, contain works by both Italian and French composers who were probably active together at the court of Avignon; during the time when the Popes resided there, Avignon was a center of secular as well as of sacred art. The Modena Codex, which includes *Notes pour moi*, was copied in the early fifteenth century, although the compositions in it probably all date from the late fourteenth century. The style of the music it contains is predominantly French, even those pieces by Italian composers such as Caserta; and the language of the texts is almost exclusively French. The forms used, too, are French —the three important "fixed forms" of the ballade, virelai, and rondeau —the majority of the compositions being in the form of the ballade.

The fourteenth-century ballade has a design similar to the ballade of the troubadour Bernart de Ventadorn (Example 6 of this book); however, the polyphonic ballade of Caserta differs in two important respects from the earlier example: it has a fourth section, so that the over-all plan is *A, A, B, C;* and it is not a rounded ballade—that is, there is no reference to previous material in the music following sections *A, A*. The texture of *Notes pour moi* is common to a great many contemporary secular works; there are two lower instrumental parts (called "tenor" and "contratenor" in this period) of similar neutral character above which a contrasting, lyrical vocal part (called "superius") stands in melodic relief. The two lower voices frequently cross each other, but never cross the upper voice, though at times they briefly touch it.

The most striking aspect of the composition is its subtle and complex rhythm, and in this respect it is representative of the spirit of rhythmical experimentation which characterized much of the music of the late fourteenth century. It is notated in such a way that the two lower voices are in duple time against a cross rhythm of the upper part in 6/8 time; the basic beat of the upper part is one-half again as long as the basic beat of the lower parts. Therefore, two bars of the upper part are equal in time to three bars of the lower voices. An additional rhythmical complication is the use of extended passages of syncopation, particularly in the upper part, as in measures 7–8, 14–16, 22–24, and other places. As a consequence, a very elaborate and intricate rhythm prevails and the various voices coincide only at widely-separated cadence points (for example, in the first section at bars 10, 16, and 19); between these points the voices move with a high degree of independence.

The cadence formula most commonly used in the composition is one in which the two lower voices move from the interval of the third outward in opposite motion to the fifth, while the upper voice moves downward from the leading tone to the sixth degree of the scale before rising to the tonic; see, for example, the final cadence of the piece. This came to be called the *Landini cadence*, although it was in use before the time of the composer for whom it is named, and continued in common use into the early fifteenth century. The open triad continues to be the chord with which practically all phrases are begun and ended.

The text, translated:

Put in music this ballad for me,
My very sweet and gracious friend!

I feel myself rather unwell,
For I have caught the grievous sickness of love.

For love of God, have pity on me,
And if you give me medicine
Let it be for true love!

Source: Modena, Biblioteca Estense, Ms. Lat. 568, fol. 13v.
Modern edition: W. Apel: *French Secular Music of the Late Fourteenth Century*, p. 29, Cambridge, 1950.

## 17. Anthonello de Caserta, Ballade, *Notes pour moi*

25
teus, Et si me
30
don me - di - ci
35
ne, Mais
40
que ce soit pour a - mour
45
fi - ne.

# 18. John Dunstable
## Isorhythmic Motet, *Veni Sancte Spiritus*

Although this motet by Dunstable was referred to previously as the last of the medieval examples in this book, it might have been as justifiably called the first of the Renaissance examples, for it combines characteristics of both epochs. The late medieval style is apparent in the *isorhythmic* ("same rhythm") structure of the work, while its Renaissance character is manifest in a use of consonance and dissonance which makes it markedly different from our previous polyphonic examples.

Dunstable, who appears to have spent a good deal of his life on the Continent, was credited even in his lifetime with having greatly influenced his contemporaries, Dufay and Binchois. His style was marked by the English predilection for fullness of sound through the use of triads and chains of sixth chords (an incorporation into written composition of the improvised practice of English discant), and by a new concept of dissonance that emerged in English music in the early fifteenth century. Before this time, the prevailing technique of composition was based on the principle that each voice had to be consonant with only one of the others (see the commentary to Example 12); the new English manner was to have each voice consonant with all the others. The principal kind of dissonance in the new style was the *suspension*—one tone of an interval or chord is temporarily held while the other tone or tones proceed to the next interval or chord; an example is seen in measure 5 of Example 18. Although other types of dissonance were used, they were chiefly for melodic and especially cadential ornamentation.

The motet *Veni Sancte Spiritus* for Pentecost, or Whitsunday (see commentary to Example 4) is one of thirty motets by Dunstable, twelve of which are isorhythmic. In the isorhythmic motet, the great art form of the fourteenth century, the tenor cantus firmus was laid out in a rhythmical pattern, sometimes fairly extended, which was reiterated through the course of the piece. This was an extension of the modal patterns used in the tenors of thirteenth-century motets, such as those of Examples 10 and 11 of this book. The isorhythmic principle continued in use in the motets of the early fifteenth century and was often exploited with great ingenuity, as it is here. In Example 18 isorhythm is confined chiefly to the tenor, which is a cantus firmus on the first phrase of the sequence for Pentecost, *Sancti Spiritus assit* (or *adsit*), quoted at the end of this commentary. This phrase is accompanied by the following canon (that is, "rule"): *Et dicitur primo directe, secundo subverte, tertio reverte mittendo terciam partem et capies dyapenthe si vis habere tenorem,* that is, the same melody is to be performed first as written [bars 10–20], then inverted [bars 41–62], then in retrograde motion and at a distance of a fifth below [bars 72–90]. Each time it occurs the tenor melody has the same rhythmic pattern it had in its first appearance, although in the third section it is in duple meter, which the motet as a whole takes on at the beginning of this section (bar 63). In the first section the tenor is sometimes between and sometimes below the other two voices, and in the last section (marked by the change to duple meter) it is entirely below. Since only the first phrase of the plainsong tenor is used, it is likely that the text with which it is underlaid is to be regarded as an incipit indicating its source, and that the entire tenor part was intended for instrumental performance. This assumption is supported when the rhythmical movement of this part is compared to the other two, each of which was doubtless intended for solo voice.

Isorhythm is only partly used in the other two voices; it occurs at the beginning of the second section (bar 32) where these voices proceed for ten bars in the same rhythm they each had at the beginning of the first section. The uppermost part has a characteristic melodic flow, with occasional cadences of the Landini type, sometimes with slight melodic and rhythmic variation.

The text used is the so-called "Golden Sequence" of the Mass for Whitsunday. (The melody of this sequence—*Veni Sancte Spiritus*—is not used by Dunstable in the motet.) The original text consists of five stanzas (see *LU*, p. 880); Dunstable employs stanzas one, four, and five as text for the uppermost voice, and stanzas two and three for the other free part. The discrepancy between the number of stanzas used in each of these two parts is caused by the fact that the lower voice proceeds generally in larger note values and somewhat more melismatically than does the upper part; the result is that while the upper voice sings one stanza for each of the three natural divisions of the composition, in the lower voice stanza two runs over to bar 41 in the second section, where stanza three begins.

The translation given is the one in *Hymns Ancient and Modern*, which is based on Edward Caswall's rendering in *Lyra Catholica* (1849).

1. Come, thou Holy Spirit, come!
And from thy celestial home
Shed a ray of light divine!
Come, thou Father of the poor!
Come, thou source of all our store!
Come, within our bosoms shine!

2. Thou, of comforters the best;
Thou, the soul's most welcome guest;
Sweet refreshment here below;
In our labor, rest most sweet;
Grateful coolness in the heat;
Solace in the midst of woe.

3. O most blessed Light divine,
Shine within these hearts of thine,
And our inmost being fill!
Where thou art not, man hath naught,
Nothing good in deed or thought,
Nothing free from taint of ill.

4. Heal our wounds, our strength renew;
On our dryness pour thy dew;
Wash the stains of guilt away:
Bend the stubborn heart and will;
Melt the frozen, warm the chill;
Guide the steps that go astray.

5. On the faithful, who adore
And confess thee, evermore
In thy sev'nfold gift descend;
Give them virtue's sure reward;
Give them thy salvation, Lord;
Give them joys that never end.

The plainsong phrase on which the tenor of the motet is based (see *Variae Preces*, Solesmes, 1901, p. 160):

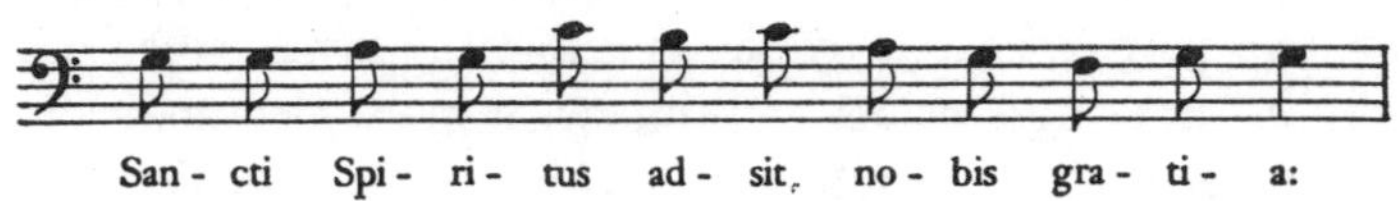
San - cti Spi - ri - tus ad - sit, no - bis gra - ti - a:

("May the grace of the Holy Spirit be with us")

Source: Trent Codices 92, No. 1543, fol. 192v–193.

Modern editions: G. Adler and O. Koller, *Trienter Codices, DTÖ*, Vol. 14–15, p. 201, Vienna, 1900. The version in this present volume is reprinted from *MB*, Vol. VIII, p. 92, *Complete Works of John Dunstable*, ed. by M. Bukofzer, © 1953, with the permission of the Royal Musical Association, the American Musicological Society, and Stainer & Bell, Ltd.

## 18. John Dunstable (d. 1453)

## Isorhythmic Motet, *Veni Sancte Spiritus*

La - va quod est sor - di - dum, ri -
35
in ae - stu tem - pe - - ri - es,
ga quod est a - - ri - dum, sa - na quod
40
la - ti - um. O lux
in fle - tu so -
est sau - ci - um. Fle - cte
45
be - a - tis - si - ma, re -
quod est ri - - - gi - dum, fo -
50
- ple cor - - dis in - ti - - ma
- ve quod est fri - gi - - - dum, re -
55
tu - o - - - -

ge quod est de - vi - - um.
rum fi - de - li - um :
Da tu - is fi - de - li - bus, in te con-fi-den-ti - bus sa-crum se-pte
Si - - ne tu - - - - - o nu - - -
- na - ri - um; Da vir - tu - tis
- mi - ne ni - hil est in
me - ri - tum , da sa - lu - tis
lu - mi - ne, ni - hil est
ex - i - tum, da pe - ren - ne gau - - di - um.
in - no - - - xi - um.

# 19. Juan del Encina
## Villancico, *Soy contento y vos servido*

This is the first of a group of four compositions (Examples 19 through 22) that represent various phases of secular music of the late fifteenth and early sixteenth centuries. The first of these—the *villancico, Soy contento*—is the Spanish equivalent of the French virelai and the Italian ballata, to which it is akin in form (see *M of M,* Nos. 4 and 10). The name *villancico* is said to derive from the Spanish *villano* ("rustic," "peasant"), indicating its origin as a song of folk source. The distinctive villancico of the late fifteenth century, however, has little of folk character, although in comparison with much of the polyphonic art music of the period it has a comely simplicity of style.

*Soy contento* is characteristic of the majority of villancicos in its prevalently chordal style, lightly broken by fleeting passages of imitation and by ornamented cadences. Typical of villancico style, also, are the predominating melody in the upper voice, the brevity of the piece, and the three-part texture—although some are in four voices, and a few in two.

Theoretically, this piece is in the (transposed) Dorian mode (Hypodorian in the upper voice), but tonal feeling is rather definitely suggested, principally through the clearly articulated tonic and dominant cadences. The texture is prevalently homophonic, and the use of dissonance is confined to the suspension. The phrasing is clear-cut, though nicely asymmetrical. It is the earliest example in this book in which tonal harmonic character is clearly foreshadowed.

The fixed form of the villancico has an over-all musical design of *A, B, B, A*. The first *A* in *Soy contento* ends at the double bar, measure 28; this is in the nature of an introductory refrain—a long one, because of the quatrain stanza—and is called the *estribillo.* The *B* section, which is repeated, and to which the second quatrain is sung, is the strophe, or *mudanza* ("change"); the last *A* is the *vuelta* ("return") which musically is a repetition of the estribillo to the text of the third quatrain. It will be noted that the last two lines of verse are the same for the estribillo as for the vuelta, which is typical of most villancicos. (The formal design of this villancico should be compared with the cantiga, *Gran dereit'*, Example 7 of this book.) The middle stanza—referred to above as the mudanza—was sometimes called the *copla,* and some villancicos have more than one copla; when this occurs the form is *A, B, B, A, B, B, A,* and so on.

The poem, translated:

*Estribillo*
I am content to serve you
Even though my fate is
That I should seek death
Rather than live without you.

*Mudanza*
I should rather be sad because of you,
Because I am irrevocably yours,
Than enjoy pleasure
Without the hope of love.

*Vuelta*
Do not think my faith lost,
For I hold it so strongly
That I should seek death
Rather than live without you.

Source: Madrid, Biblioteca Real, *Cancionero Musical de Palacio,* 2-1-5, fols. 37–38.

Modern editions: F. Barbieri, *Cancionero Musical Español de los Siglos XV y XVI,* No. 40, Madrid, 1890. H. Anglès, *La Musica en la Corte de los Reyes Catolicos,* II, No. 50, Barcelona, 1947.

## 19. Juan del Encina, Villancico, *Soy contento y vos servido*

# 20. Marchetto Cara
## Frottola, *O mia cieca e dura sorte*

The *frottola* arose in the courts of northern Italy—notably at Mantua—contemporaneously with the Spanish villancico. This example is from the earliest printed book of *frottole* (Petrucci, Venice, 1504), which contains works in this genre by Cara, Pesenti, and Tromboncini, the three outstanding Italian frottola composers. The frottola is a musical form of considerable historical significance because it was the immediate forerunner of the madrigal, and because *frottole* composers came to use four-part writing and a harmonically-conceived chordal texture. This frottola, as written by Cara, is given as the music on the two upper staves of Example 20–21; the lowest staff is a lute arrangement of this same composition from the Capirola lute book, probably written about ten years later than the original version. The two pieces are arranged together only so they can be easily compared; they are not intended to be performed together. (Compare these two examples with A. Gabrieli's harpsichord transcription of Crequillon's chanson, *M of M*, Nos. 20 and 21.)

Aside from the use of four parts, the texture of *O mia cieca* is not very different from that of the villancico of Example 19, although the underlying chordal character of the frottola is more strongly emphasized by its rhythmical definiteness and its predominating four-bar phrasing. As in the villancico, imitation is used sparingly (note the brief passage in the three lower voices at measure 15). Melodic interest is confined to the top voice; the bass has many leaps of 8ves, 4ths, and 5ths, and the inner parts are mere harmonic filling in almost throughout the piece.

The form of the frottola is very like that of the villancico. It has an opening *ripresa* ("refrain"), which in Example 20 is the section up to the double bar at measure 20 set to a text of four lines. This is followed by the *piede,* or stanza, which is usually, as here, a six-line verse, going from the double bar to the end of the piece. Then comes the *volta* ("return," *cf.* Spanish *vuelta*), which is the return to the beginning of the composition, and which consists of the same text and music as the ripresa. Most *frottole* have several piedi, and these could be continued in the song in two different ways ($R =$ ripresa, $P =$ piedi, $V =$ volta): 1) $R, P^1, V, R, P^2, V$, etc.; or 2) $R, P^1, V, P^2, V$, etc. The lines of the text (four in the ripresa, six in the piede) correspond generally to the musical phrases; but the text is not repeated, except for the last half-line of each of these sections. The musical phrases, however, have the following melodic design: Ripresa = *a, b, b, c, c;* piede = *d, e, e, b, b, c.* Because of the special arrangement of Example 20–21 on the page, the successive piedi have not been put at the appropriate places in the music, as have previous examples of strophic compositions in this book, but separately at the end of the music. Incidentally, this is the way in which they appear in the original source. The translation of the entire text appears at the end of the commentary to Example 21.

The poetry of the frottola texts is in general not of the highest literary quality, although it has an undeniable vitality. The principal theme is love; and the *frottole* have been regarded as a repertory of lovers' serenades, compositions for use in any possible kind of amorous occasion—*Rime della vita cortigiana* ("Verses for use in court life"). They range in mood from the satirical to the highly sentimental; this particular frottola is one of the sentimental ones.

# 21. Vincenzo Capirola
# Lute Transcription, *O mia cieca e dura sorte*

Music for the lute formed an important part of Renaissance instrumental music. In addition to dances and pieces in both strict and improvisatory styles, considerable use was made of arrangements in lute idiom of existing vocal models, such as that seen on the lowest staff of Example 20–21. The Capirola lute book, from which it is taken, is the earliest known manuscript of lute music, although it is antedated by a printed lute book—Petrucci's *Intabolatura de lauto*, 1507—by about a decade.

Lute music was written in a special kind of notation called *tablature*, a sort of "finger notation" in which a staff-like set of six lines representing the six strings of the lute carried letters or numbers which represented the frets to be stopped by the left hand. Rhythm was indicated by stems and flags above the lines and notes. The system was simple, direct, and effective, and remained in use throughout the active period of the lute. (The tablature system may be seen in the Gaulthier *Tombeau*, Example 39 of this book.) Tablature notation for the lute presents a special problem to the modern transcriber, who must decide whether to render the music literally as it appears in the tablature—which indicates only the point where a tone or chord is played—or to write out the voice-leading where it is implied by holding tones where they might have been held. The first, literal method has been adopted for the accompanying example. (The same piece transcribed in the second manner may be seen in O. Gombosi's edition of the Capirola lute book, p. 10. See also the accompaniment of the Dowland lute song, Example 34 of this book.)

A comparison of the original vocal model with the lute arrangement shows the usual technique employed in such arrangements. The addition of melodic embellishments—turns, appoggiaturas, passing tones, scale passages, a brief introductory flourish, and ornamental cadences—are the principal changes made. Beyond this there is an occasional change of harmony (bars 5, 7, and 9); and where desirable, a repeated chord is sometimes omitted in the instrumental piece (bars 4 and 24), although the opposite procedure also occurs, and a single chord of the frottola is repeated in the transcription (bars, 8, 12, 35, and 36).

It will be seen in this example that in a great many places the two versions do not correspond in the matter of accidentals. It is likely that in the performance of the frottola at the period in which it was written the same use of accidentals would be made by the performers of each version, although this is not certain.

The translation of the text:

*Ripresa*

O my blind and cruel fate,
Continually nourished by sorrow,
O misery that is my life—
Sad harbinger of my death.

*Piedi*

1. I am more sorrowful and unhappy
Than anyone who lives;
I am the tree the wind blows down
Because it no longer has roots.
It is well and truly said that
Evil walks with him who has an evil destiny.

2. The cause of so many ills
Is fortune and cruel love.
Because I have always served
Immortal faith with all my heart
It has broken my wings,
And bound me on every side.

3. For him who has a hard and heavy life,
A hard and heavy death is suitable.
I want to end in tears and pain,
Like a ship that goes on a reef,
Which breaks all its beams at last
In the violent storm.

4. Take heed, every one who sees it
Written on my dark tomb.
Though I am beyond nature,
I have died through too much faith.
For me there was never mercy;
Pity closes the doors on me.

Sources: O. Petrucci, *Frottole Libro Primo*, Venice, 1504. Newberry Library, Chicago, *The Capirola Lute Manuscript* (*ca.* 1515).

Modern editions: R. Schwartz, *Ottaviano Petrucci, Frottole, Books I and IV*, p. 3, Leipzig, 1935. R. Monterosso, *Frottole nell'edizione principe di O. Petrucci*, Cremona, 1954. Contains facsimile reproductions of several frottole from the Petrucci prints. O. Gombosi, *Compositione di Meser Vincenzo Capirola*, Paris, 1955. Contains several facsimile pages, some in color.

## 20. Marchetto Cara, Frottola, *O mia cieca e dura sorte*

## 21. Vincenzo Capirola, Lute Transcription, *O mia cieca e dura sorte*

vi- - ta, Tris - to a - nun-tio a la
15 mi- a mor - - te, a la mia
mor - - te.
20
(Fine)
Piu do-
len- te e in- - fe - li - - ce

25
Son, che al - cun che vi - va in
ter - - ra; ar - bor son, chel
30
ven - to at - ter - ra, Per che piu non ha ra -
35
di - - ce. Ver e ben quel,

che se di - - ce:
40
Che mal va, chi ha ma - la sor - te, chi ha
ma - la sor - te.
45
(D.C.)

# 22. Hans Sachs
## Meistersinger Melody, *Gesangweise*

It is significant that the *Meistergesang* of Hans Sachs is the sole example of monophonic music among the Renaissance compositions in this book, as it represents an art that musically was a direct continuation of the medieval monophonic Minnelied. It was an art that became obsolete not long after the time when this song was written, however; it had remained an isolated phenomenon, untouched by the vigorous musical activity of the fifteenth and sixteenth centuries, and had lost the lyrical freshness of feeling characteristic of most of the Minnesinger pieces.

The Meistersinger were craftsmen and businessmen, solid bourgeoisie who cultivated music as an avocation to which they applied rules similar to those that governed their trades; thus a beginner at music could rise through the ranks from *Schüler* (apprentice) to *Meister*, one who was able to compose both music and poetry. The trial by which aspirants were judged, according to the stiff and formal rules of the *Tabulatur*, is amusingly and accurately portrayed in Wagner's *Die Meistersinger*.

The *Gesangweise* of Hans Sachs, the famed shoemaker-poet of Nuremberg, has a text which is Biblical, like most of the Meistersinger texts; the piece itself is nonliturgical, of course. The poem consists of a rhymed paraphrase of the opening verses of the Ninety-fourth Psalm; a characteristic opening sentence cites the source of the text. The melody is in the Hypophrygian mode, and is cast in the typical Minnesinger *Barform* of two *Stollen* followed by an *Abgesang* (see *M of M*, No. 5). Halfway through the Abgesang (end of bar 23) there is a return to the melody of the Stollen, slightly modified. Also characteristic of the Meistersinger art are the *Blumen*, or melodic embellishments—the cadenza-like beginning and the return to the Stollen melody in bar 23, and the occasional lesser melodic decorations which occur throughout the rest of the composition.

The rhythm of the Meistersinger melodies presents a special problem. The Meistersinger scribes retained the type of Gothic notation used by the Minnesinger in which there is no indication of rhythm, even though mensural notation was highly developed at the time when Hans Sachs was active. The only clue to the rhythm lies in the nature of the text, which is in what Adam Puschmann (the last of the Meistersinger and a pupil of Hans Sachs) referred to as "Meistersinger" verse; the number of syllables per line is irregular, but the number of syllables in parallel lines of the Stollen is the same. Accentuation was a matter of indifference, however, so that there is often a clash between the natural accents of text and melody, and although word accents may correspond to melodic accents in certain parts of one Stollen, they often do not in the equivalent places in the other. Scholars once attempted to force these melodies into a four-beat, four-measure-phrase pattern, but a more recent approach, used in this transcription, allows a freer, more declamatory manner.

The opening line of text might be translated as: "Hear, ye Christians, a Psalm in song, the fine ninety-fourth one," after which follows a fairly close rendering of the first eight verses and first half of the ninth verse, which in the King James version read as follows:

1. O Lord God, to whom vengeance belongeth; O God, to whom vengeance belongeth, shew thyself.
2. Lift up thyself, thou judge of the earth: render a reward to the proud.
3. Lord, how long shall the wicked, how long shall the wicked triumph?
4. How long shall they utter and speak hard things? and all the workers of iniquity boast themselves?
5. They break in pieces thy people, O Lord, and afflict thine heritage.
6. They slay the widow and the stranger, and murder the fatherless.
7. Yet they say, the Lord shall not see, neither shall the God of Jacob regard it.
8. Understand, ye brutish among the people; and, ye fools, when will ye be wise?
9. He that planted the ear, shall he not hear?

Source: *Das Singebuch des Adam Puschmann* (1532–1600).
Modern edition: G. Münzer, *Das Singebuch des Adam Puschmann*, p. 77, Leipzig, 1906.

## 22. Hans Sachs (1494–1576)

### Meistersinger Melody, *Gesangweise*

# 23. Cristobal Morales
## *Magnificat Octavi Toni*

This composition is the first of a series of six pieces (Examples 23–28) which illustrate different phases of sixteenth-century sacred composition, both Catholic and Protestant. The work by Morales is for the Roman liturgy of the Office of Vespers, the last but one of the daily Hours, which provides for a greater use of music than any of the other Offices; except for the Mass, it is the only service of the Roman Church in which music other than plainchant may be sung. The structure of Vespers comprises the Introit *Deus in adjutorium*, five Psalms with Antiphons, a seasonal Hymn, and the crowning musical offering of the Magnificat. The text of the Magnificat is the Canticle of the Virgin Mary to Elizabeth after the angel Gabriel had announced that she would become the Mother of Jesus (Luke 1:46–55).

The usual manner in which sixteenth-century composers set the twelve verses of the text is illustrated in this notable example by the Spanish *maestro de capilla* and one time member of the Papal Choir, Cristobal Morales. In it, the even-numbered verses are composed polyphonically for performance by a small group of soloists; the odd-numbered verses are intended to be sung in plainchant by the choir. Morales, like many of his contemporaries, wrote a complete set of sixteen Magnificats (two in each mode); eight of these treat the odd-numbered verses polyphonically, and the other eight treat the even-numbered verses polyphonically.

Morales employed the reciting tone to which the plainchant verses are sung as a cantus firmus for the polyphonic sections. (The Solemn Tone of the eighth mode is given at the beginning of Example 23.) The plainchant appears in unadorned form as the soprano of verse two (bar 5), the bass of verse four (bar 26), the alto of verse six (bar 43), the tenor of verse eight (bar 68), and the soprano in verse ten (bar 89). In the last verse a fuller texture is created by the addition of two voices—an alto and a tenor; the plainchant appears here as a canon between alto II (the upper part of the middle staff, bar 105) and tenor II (upper part, lower staff, bar 108).

Around this golden thread is woven a beautifully clear and transparent polyphony that is predominantly one of free imitation, the motives of which are themselves derived from the chant theme. A structural feature of most verses is the careful observance by the composer of the two segments into which the verses naturally fall; the beginning of each verse is set to the rising figure with which the chant begins, while the second part begins with the repeated-note figure derived from the iteration of the reciting-note at the beginning of the second half of the chant (for example, bars 1 and 14 in verse two, bars 21 and 33 in verse four, and bars 63 and 75 of verse eight). The prevailing flow of imitative writing is occasionally contrasted with short stretches of chordal writing; the beginning of one verse—the sixth—is in a straightforward chordal style. The harmony is modal in the sense that it does not clearly define tonal relationships; but it displays a trend toward tonality by the emphasis given the cadences, at which the bass line takes on a character different from the other voices.

The glorious fullness of the six-voiced final verse brings the composition to a climactic intensity of mystical fervor which is heightened in the final *Amen* section by the several upward-thrusting octave leaps.

The translation of the Magnificat as it appears in the Order for Daily Evening Prayer in the *Book of Common Prayer* (p. 26) is as follows; the verses are arranged according to traditional Roman usage.

1. My soul doth magnify the Lord.
2. And my spirit hath rejoiced in God my Saviour.
3. For he hath regarded the lowliness of his handmaiden. For behold, from henceforth all generations shall call me blessed.
4. For he that is mighty hath magnified me; and holy is his name.
5. And his mercy is on them that fear him throughout all generations.
6. He hath showed strength with his arm; he hath scattered the proud in the imagination of their hearts.
7. He hath put down the mighty from their seat, and hath exalted the humble and the meek.
8. He hath filled the hungry with good things, and the rich he hath sent empty away.

9. He remembering his mercy hath holpen his servant Israel.
10. As he promised to our forefathers, Abraham and his seed, for ever.
11. Glory be to the Father, and to the Son, and to the Holy Ghost.
12. As it was in the beginning, is now, and ever shall be, world without end, Amen.

The chant to which the odd-numbered verses of the *Magnificat* are sung (see *LU*, p. 218):

The Latin texts of the odd-numbered verses are as follows:

3. Quia respexit humilitatem ancillae suae: ecce enim ex hoc beatam me dicent omnes generationes.
5. Et misericordia ejus a progenie in progenies timentibus eum.
7. Deposuit potentes de sede, et exaltavit humiles.
9. Suscepit Israel puerum suum, recordatus misericordiae suae.
11. Gloria Patri, et Filio, et Spiritui Sancto.

Source: *Magnificat Moralis Ispanicum quatuor vocibus, Liber primus.* Printed by Ant. Gardane, Venice, 1545.

Modern editions: H. Anglès, *Cristobal de Morales, Opera Omnia*, Vol. IV, p. 126, Barcelona, 1956. P. Pedrell, *Hispaniae Schola Musica Sacra*, Vol. I, p. 20, Barcelona, 1894.

# 23. Cristobal Morales (*ca.* 1500–1553)

## *Magnificat Octavi Toni*

ri me - - - - - - o.
20
o, in De - o sa - lu - ta - ri - me - o.
o, in De - o sa – lu - ta - ri me - - - o.
sa - lu - ta - ri me - - - - - o.
Qui - a fe - cit mi -
Qui - a fe - cit mi -
3. Quia respexit
4. Qui - a fe - cit mi - hi ma - - gna, mi -
hi ma - gna qui po - tens
25
– hi ma - gna qui po - tens
– hi ma - gna qui pot - ens est,
Qui - a fe -
est, mi - hi mag - na qui po -
30
est, qui pot - ens est
mi - hi ma - gna qui po - tens est; et
- cit mi - hi ma - gna qui
tens est: et san - ctum no - men e -
: et san- ctum no - men e - - - -
san - ctum no - men e - jus, et san-ctum
pot - ens est:

jus ———, no - men e - jus, et ——— san - ctum no - men
35
jus, et san - ctum no - men e -
no - - men e - jus, et san - ctum no - men
et san - ctum no - men e - jus,
e - - - - - jus.
40
- jus, no - men ——— e - jus . ———
e jus, no - men e - jus.
et san - ctum no - men e - - jus.
Fe - cit po - ten - ti - am in
45
5. Et misericordia
6. Fe - cit po - ten - ti - am in
Fe - cit po - ten - ti - am in
Fe - cit po - ten - ti - am in
bra - - chi - o su - - o : ———
50
bra - chi - o su - - o:
bra - - chi - o su - - o: di -
bra - - chi - o ——— su - - o: di -
——— di - sper - sit su - per - bos men - te
di - sper - sit su - per - bos ——— men -
sper - sit su - per - bos men - te cor - dis ——— su -
sper - sit su - per - - bos men - te cor - dis

cor - dis su - - - i, men - te
55
- te cor - dis su - i, men - te
- i, su - - - i,
su - i, men - te cor -
cor - dis su - - - i.
60
cor - dis su - i .
men - te cor - dis su - i.
dis su - i, su - - - i.
65
E - su - ri -
7. Deposuit
8. E - su - ri - en - tes im - ple - vit bo -
E - su - ri - en - tes im - ple -vit
en - tes im - ple - - vit bo -
nis, im - ple - vit bo -
E - su - -
bo - - - nis,
- - nis, im - ple - vit bo -
70
- - nis, im - ple - vit bo -
ri - - en - tes im - ple - vit bo - -
E - su - ri - en - - - tes im - ple - vit

- nis: et di- vi- tes di - -
75
- nis: et di- vi- tes di- mi - -
- - - - - nis: et di- vi-
bo- nis: et di- vi- tes di- mi- sit
mi- sit in- a - - nes, et di- vi-
80
sit, di- mi- sit in- a- nes, et di- vi-
tes di- mi- sit in- a - - -
in - a - - nes, et di- vi-
tes di- mi- sit in - a - - -
tes di- mi- sit in- a- nes, di-
nes, et di- vi- tes di- mi-
tes di- mi- sit in - -
nes, di- mi- sit in - a - nes.
85
- mi- sit in- a - - nes.
sit in - - a - - nes.
- nes, in- a - - nes.
Si - cut lo- cu-
90
Sic - ut lo - cu - tus est ad pa-
9. Suscepit Israel
10. Sic - ut lo - cu - tus est ad
Sic - ut lo - cu - tus est ad pa-

- tus est ad pa - tres no - -
- tres no - stros, ad pa - tres no -
pa - - - - tres
- tres no - stros, ad pa - tres
stros, A - -
95
- stros, A - bra - ham, et
no - stros, A - bra - ham
no - stros, A - bra - ham, et
- bra - ham, et se - mi - ni e - jus
100
se - mi - ni e - jus, et se - mi-ni e -
et se - - mi - ni e -
se - mi - ni e - jus, et se - mi -
in sae - cu - la.
jus in sae - cu - la.
- jus in sae - - cu - la.
ni e - jus in sae - cu - la.

Cum sex vocibus
Sic - ut e -
105
Sic - - ut
Canon in Diapente
11. Gloria Patri
12. Sic - ut e - rat
Sic - ut e - rat, sic - ut e -
Resolutio
Sic - ut
Sic - ut e - - rat,
rat in prin - ci - -
110
e - - - rat in
in prin - ci - pi - o,
- rat in prin-ci - pi - o
e - rat in prin-
sic - ut e - rat in
- pi - o, et nunc, et sem - -
115
prin - ci - pi - o, et nunc et
et nunc, et sem -
et nunc, et sem - per,
ci - pi - o,
prin - ci - pi - o, et nunc, et

per,
et nunc et sem -
120
sem - - - per, et nunc, et
per,
et nunc et sem - per, et sem -
et nunc et sem - per,
sem - per, et nunc, et sem - per,
- per, et in sae - cu - la sae - - cu -
125
sem - per, et in sae cu - la sae - cu - lo -
et in sae - cu - la
per, et in sae - cu - la sae -
et in
et in sae - cu - la sae - cu -
lo - rum. A - - - - - - - -
rum. A men, sae - cu - lo - rum. A men, sae - cu - - lo -
sae - cu - lo rum. A - men,
cu - lo - - rum, sae - cu - lo - rum. A - -
sae - cu la
lo - rum. A - men, sae - cu -

men, sae - cu - lo - -
130
rum. A - - men, sae -
sae - cu -
- - - - - men,
sae - cu lo - rum. A - men,
lo - rum. A - men, sae -
- - - rum. A - men, sae -
135
cu - lo - rum, sae - cu - lo -
lo - - rum. A - men,
sae - cu - lo - rum. A - men, sae -
sae - cu -
cu - lo - rum. A - men,
cu - lo - rum. A - - men.
- rum. A - - - men.
A - men.
- - cu - lo - rum. A - - - men.
lo - - rum. A - - men.
sae - cu - lo - rum. A - men.

# 24. Johann Walter
## Chorale, *Komm, Gott Schöpfer, heiliger Geist*

This chorale and the examples that immediately follow it are among the earliest manifestations of Protestant music as it emerged in the sixteenth century in the German Reformation, in Calvinism in France, and in the Church of England. The first of these examples, the *Geistliche Gesang* of Johann Walter, *Komm, Gott Schöpfer, heiliger Geist*, has associations that cut across many centuries of Western culture. Its direct origin, in both melody and text, is the hymn for Whitsunday, *Veni Creator Spiritus*, which is Example 4 of this book (see the commentary there). The text of Walter's setting is a German translation of the hymn made by Martin Luther. The composition first appeared in the original edition of Walter's *Geystliche Gesangk Buchleyn* (Wittenberg, 1524), the first published collection of choral music for the new liturgy, and it remained in all four subsequent revised editions of that famous collection with some slight refinements in the counterpoint made by Walter himself. The reading of Example 24 is from the edition of 1551. (An English translation of Luther's foreword to the *Geystliche Gesangk Buchleyn* is given in *SR*, p. 341.)

Although there are certain differences in melodic and harmonic style, and especially in texture, between Walter's setting of *Komm, Gott Schöpfer* and Morales' *Magnificat* (Example 23), they show a general similarity of organization: in both pieces the plainchant melody serves as a long-note cantus firmus around which the other voices weave imitative counterpoint. In Example 24, the hymn melody is stated in its entirety; the first of its four phrases appears in the tenor in the opening section (bar 4), after which it moves to the soprano and remains in that voice during the rest of the piece; the beginnings of phrases two, three, and four are seen at bars 18, 29, and 45, respectively.

The contrapuntal play of voices follows an interesting musical design. In the first section, all four voices take part in a fugato on the chant melody, the two lower voices presenting it in unadorned fashion and in close canonic imitation. In the second phrase, the cantus melody is preceded by an entry of the head of the theme in the tenor (bar 16), but the counterpoint in the other voices remains free. In the third phrase, the chant is introduced by preceding entries in tenor and alto in close imitation and in diminution (bars 27 and 28), the bass being free. The last phrase of the cantus is ushered in by preceding imitation in all the other voices in diminution (bars 41 and 42). Thus a cumulative effect is achieved, which is heightened by the manner in which the last section begins; it is the only one before which the preceding section ends cadentially, since the separations between phrases in the other sections have been smoothly overlapped by the continuing motion of the lower voices.

The sectional character and fugato style employed in this piece make it resemble a motet form upon which a long-note cantus has been superimposed; this description would apply to about half of the forty-three compositions in the Wittenberg songbook. It should be added, though, that nearly all these have the cantus in the tenor; the present example is somewhat exceptional in having the principal melody in the upper voice for the greater part of the piece. Another category of pieces in Walter's book consists of pieces in chordal style, with the cantus in the tenor; these pieces were the direct forerunners of the Lutheran chorales.

Walter follows the melody of *Veni Creator Spiritus* fairly closely, as a note-by-note comparison of that tune with the cantus melody of *Komm, Gott Schöpfer* will reveal. Almost the only modifications are the occasional extensions of phrase-endings. As the melody came to be used as a congregational chorale tune, however, its outline was made simpler, and its character more four-square. These changes are illustrated in other versions from the sixteenth, seventeenth, and eighteenth centuries, all of which use Luther's translation as text:

The translation of the verse set by Walter (verse 1):

Come, O Creator Spirit, come,
And make within our hearts thy home:
To us thy Grace celestial give,
Who of thy breathing move and live.

Source: *Geystliche Gesanck Buchleyn*, No. 2, Wittenberg, 1524.
Modern editions: O. Kade, *Johann Walter, Wittembergische Geistliche Gesangbuch von 1524*, p. 67, Berlin, 1878. O. Schröder, *Johann Walter, Sämtliche Werke*, I, p. 4, Kassel, 1953.

# 24. Johann Walter (1496–1570)

## Chorale, *Komm, Gott Schöpfer, heiliger Geist*

Herz der Men - -
Herz der Men - -
- - - - - - - -
der - Men - - - - - - -
schen dein
- - - schen dein mit
- schen dein mit Gna -
- schen dein mit Gna - - -
mit Gna - - - den
Gna - - - - - - den
den sie füll, wie
- den sie
sie füll,
sie füll, wie
du weisst,
füll, wie du weisst, wie -
wie du weisst,
du weisst,
wie du weisst,
du weisst,

dass dein Ge - schöpf vor - hin sein, dass dein
dass dein Ge - - schöpf, dass dein
dass dein Ge - schöpf vor - hin
dass dein Ge - schöpf vor -
45
Ge - schöpf vor - hin
Ge - schöpf vor - hin sein, vor - - -
sein, das dein Ge - schöpf, dass dein Ge - schöpf
- hin sein
50
sein, dass dein Ge -
- - - hin sein, vor - hin
vor - hin sein, vor - - hin
55
schöpf vor - - - - - hin sein.
sein.
sein.

# 25. Claude Goudimel
## Psalm Setting, *Mon Dieu me paist*
## From the French Psalter of 1564

# 26. Claude Goudimel
## Psalm Setting, *Mon Dieu me paist*
## From the French Psalter of 1565

---

The leaders of the French Reformation turned to the Psalms as their principal texts for songs written for congregational singing; and Psalters—collections of these songs—began to be published shortly before the middle of the sixteenth century. A collection of rhymed metrical versions of all 150 Psalms by Clément Marot and Théodore de Bèze, with tunes selected and arranged by Louis Bourgeois, was published in 1542. This collection, known as the *Genevan Psalter*, was prepared under Calvin's direction; it was a work of considerable literary distinction, and greatly influenced the Dutch, German, English, and Scotch Psalters that appeared shortly thereafter. The music in the Genevan Psalter is entirely monophonic; as in the case of the Lutheran melodies, the melodies were in part adaptations of existing melodies, most of them secular in origin, though some were those used in Calvin's shorter Strasbourg Psalter of 1539. It seems likely that some of the unidentified melodies, about half the tunes, were composed by Bourgeois himself. The beginning of the tune used in the Twenty-third Psalm suggests that its origin may lie in a French chanson.

Goudimel, a convert to the Reformed church, and a victim of the St. Bartholomew massacre at Lyons in 1572, had written Roman

Catholic liturgical music of a high quality before his conversion. Examples 25 and 26 illustrate his work as a Huguenot composer, and show two part-settings of the same melody; they are placed one above the other to facilitate comparison. The setting on the upper of the two braces is from an edition of the entire Psalter written in embellished-chord style, published in Paris in 1564; the melody of the Genevan Psalter is in the uppermost part, which is true of most of the Psalms in this collection. The setting in the lower brace is one of another version by Goudimel of the entire Psalter published at Paris in 1565. The style employed in this collection is note-against-note; the original melody of the Twenty-third Psalm is in the tenor, as it is in most of the arrangements in the 1565 version. In a foreword to the 1565 collection, Goudimel states that the three parts have been added not for use in the church but in the home.[1]

The rendering of the text in this version of the beloved Twenty-third Psalm is known to be Marot's. It is a rhymed, metrical paraphrase in three stanzas. In the original edition, as here, the first stanza only is printed with the music; the other stanzas are printed separately, though as close as possible to the stanza with music, and are sung strophically to the same music. Each stanza consists of three rhymed couplets, and each of the six lines that make up the stanza is the same length—eleven syllables—being wholly unlike the Psalm text of Hans Sachs in this respect (see Example 22). Like most of the texts in the Genevan Psalter, its meter is iambic, and all the endings are feminine.

The melody, which is in the transposed Dorian mode, is one of the best in the Psalter, and was used in the Ainsworth Psalter and in some Lutheran collections of the seventeenth century. The setting of 1564 is fundamentally chordal in texture, but has some embellishing passages of imitative character at the beginnings of certain phrases—the opening of the piece; at bar 5, between soprano and alto; at the up-beat of bar 9, where there is a canonic passage of several bars between soprano and bass; and at bar 18, where a briefer passage of canon occurs between soprano and tenor. Imitation also occurs at the beginning of the

[1] The complete text of Goudimel's remark concerning this is as follows: "To the Reader: We have added three parts to the Psalm tunes in this little book, not to be sung in church, but for rejoicing in God in the home. This should not be considered wrong, since the tune as it is used in the church remains intact, as if it appeared by itself."

last phrase between tenor and soprano (bars 22 and 23), and also among bass, alto, and tenor (bars 22 and 25). Other decorative elements in the three lower parts are passages of eighth-notes, syncopations, and embellished cadences.

None of these embellishments is used in the other setting; the only deviation there from the simple note-against-note harmonization is a soprano suspension at the ends of the last two phrases (bars 21 and 26). It is noteworthy that in this setting the cadence chord at the end of all but one phrase lacks the third; the only exception is the chord in bar 17, and in this case the third is unavoidable as it is in the cantus firmus.

The King James version of the Twenty-third Psalm:

1. The Lord is my shepherd; I shall not want.
2. He maketh me to lie down in green pastures: he leadeth me beside the still waters.
3. He restoreth my soul: he leadeth me in the paths of righteousness for his name's sake.
4. Yea, though I walk through the valley of the shadow of death, I will fear no evil: for thou art with me; thy rod and thy staff they comfort me.
5. Thou preparest a table before me in the presence of mine enemies: thou anointest my head with oil; my cup runneth over.
6. Surely goodness and mercy shall follow me all the days of my life; and I will dwell in the house of the Lord for ever.

Sources: *Les cent cinquante Psaumes de David, nouvellement mis en musique à quatre parties par C. Goudimel.* Paris, 1564.
*Les Pseaumes mis en rime françoise par Clément Marot et Thèodore de Bèze. Mis en musique à quatre parties par Claude Goudimel.* Geneva, 1565. (Also printed same year at Paris.) Facsimile reprint of the above, Kassel, 1935.

Modern editions: H. Expert, *Les Maîtres Musiciens de la Renaissance Française,* Vol. IV, p. 93, Paris, 1896. After a reprint of the 1564 Psalter published in 1580. W. S. Pratt, *The Music of the French Psalter of 1562,* New York, 1939. The frontispiece of this book is a facsimile reproduction of the page of the Psalter that contains the tune of Psalm XXIII.

25. Claude Goudimel, Psalm Setting, *Mon Dieu me paist*
From the French Psalter of 1564

26. Psalm Setting, *Mon Dieu me paist*, from the French Psalter of 1565

rien je n'au - rai fau - te. En tect bien seur,
10
je n'au-rai fau - - te. En tect bien seur,
rien je n'au - rai fau - - - te. En tect bien
je n'au-rai fau - te. En tect bien seur, joi - gnant les
rien je n'au-rai fau - te. En tect bien seur,
joi - gnant les beaux her-ba - ges, cou- cher me fait, me
15
joi - gnant les beaux her- ba - ges, cou - cher me fait, me meine
seur, joi - gnant les beaux her - ba - ges, cou - cher me fait, me
beaux her- ba - - - ges, cou- cher me fait, me
joi - gnant les beaux her- ba - ges, cou - cher me fait, me

meine aux clairs ri - va - ges; trai - te ma vie
aux clairs _ ri - va - ges; trai - te ma vie en dou -
meine aux clairs ri - va - - - ges; trai- te ma vie en
meine aux clairs ri - va - ges; trai - te ma vie . en dou- ceur tres hu -
meine aux clairs ri - va - ges; trai - te ma vie
20
en dou - ceur tres hu - mai - ne, et pour son
- ceur tres hu - mai - ne, et pour son
dou - ceur tres ___ hu - mai - - ne, et pour son Nom
mai - ne, et pour son Nom, et
en dou - ceur tres hu- mai - ne, et pour son

Nom par droits sen - tiers me mei - - ne.
25
Nom par droits sen- tiers me mei - - ne.
et pour son Nom par droits sen- tiers me mei - - ne.
pour son Nom par droits sen- tiers me mei - ne.
Nom par droits sen - tiers me mei - ne.

# 27. Thomas Tallis

## Anthem, *Heare the voyce and prayer of thy servaunts*

---

As in Germany and France, the use of the vernacular quickly became established in the liturgy of the English reformed church. A royal decree specifying the use of English in church music was issued in 1548, the Sternhold-Hopkins *English Psalter* was printed in 1549, and Merbecke's *Booke of Common Praier Noted* appeared in 1550. Even before this, however, a set of nearly one hundred anthems and liturgical pieces with English words had been composed and arranged by six or more English composers. This manuscript is thought to have been written down about three or four years before the middle of the century. Part of this collection was published in London in 1560, and selections from this volume, including the Tallis example seen here, were published again in 1565. The title of the 1565 edition read: "Morning and Evenyng prayer and Communion, set forthe in four partes to be song in Churches, both for men and children, wyth dyvers other godly praiers & Anthems, of sundry meins doynges."

Example 27 is therefore one of the earliest examples of the English anthem, a sacred piece whose position in the Anglican liturgy is similar to that of the motet in the Roman church—that is, it is allowed by ecclesiastical authority, but is not an essential part of the liturgy. In the Anglican ritual the anthem was originally sung at the end of morning and evening prayer.

The sixteenth-century English anthem is hardly distinguishable in musical style from the Latin motet, although it is more syllabic and rhythmically simpler. In these respects the Tallis piece is quite representative of the early English church style.

The characteristic motet design is seen in the sectional treatment of the successive phrases of the text. Each of its five sections (bars 1, 6, 12, 19, and 24) commences with a fresh subject for each new line of text, which is carried on in imitative counterpoint. There is a considerable degree of overlapping between sections. A distinctive trait of the piece as a whole is the thematic affinity of the various subjects, brought about by the upward leap of the fourth which is present in all of them; the use of the diminished fourth in the subject of the first section is conspicuous.

The text of Tallis' piece is Biblical; it comes from the First Book of Kings, 8:28–30, and is part of Solomon's address to the assembled hosts of Israel upon the completion of the temple. Possibly an anagogical reference is intended between the building of the temple and the establishment of the new Church of England.

As the English anthem evolved in the later sixteenth and early seventeenth centuries, other features were introduced: short passages for solo voice, the use of an organ accompaniment executing the figured bass, and a more pronounced syllabic style; but English church music always maintained something of the motet character (see the Canticle setting by Blow, Example 43 of this book). Objection to the motet style was raised frequently in the sixteenth century, not only by the non-Conformist Puritans (who would have rejected part-singing of any kind), but also by some English churchmen who were greatly concerned about conveying the spiritual message of the church; they felt that the imitative style obscured the meaning of the text by "too frequent fugue"—that is, imitation—and by a disregard for the normal accentuation of the words.

Source: Oxford, Bodleian Library, E. 420–22 (the Wanley Manuscript), London, printed by John Day, 1560.

Modern editions: Charles Burney, *A General History of Music*, Vol. III, p. 27, London, 1776–89. Modern edition of Burney, ed. by F. Mercer, Vol. II, p. 33, London, 1935.

## 27. Thomas Tallis (*ca.* 1505–1585)

### Anthem, *Heare the voyce and prayer of thy servaunts*

that thine eyes may be 15 o - pen to - ward this
house night and day, this
to - ward this house night and day,
eyes may be o - pen to - ward this house night
house night and day e - ver to - ward this
house night and day e - ver to - ward this
night and day e - ver to - ward this
and day e - ver to - ward this
place, e - ver to - ward this place of
place, e - ver to - ward this place
place, e - ver to - ward this place of which thou hast
place, e - ver to - ward this place
20 which thou hast said my name shall be
of which thou hast
said my name shall be there,
of which thou hast said my name shall be
there, my name shall be there, my name shall
said my name shall be there, my name
and when thou hear'st have mer - cy
there, my name shall be there, my name

— be, there, — 25 — and when thou
shall be there, and when thou hear'st have mer - cy on —
on — them, and when thou hear'st have mer - cy
shall be there, — and when thou
hear'st have mer - cy on them, and when thou hear'st have
them, on — them, and when thou — hear'st
on them, and when thou
hear'st have mer - cy on them, and
30 mer - - - - - - cy on them, and when thou
and when thou hear'st have mer -
hear'st have mer - cy on — them, and when thou
when thou hear'st have mer - cy on them, and when thou
hear'st have mer - cy up - on them. 35
cy — on — them.
hear'st have mer - cy — on them.
hear'st have mer - cy — on — them.

# 28. Hans Leo Hassler
## Polychoral Motet, *Laudate Dominum*

*Laudate Dominum* illustrates another aspect of the Latin motet as it was written in the polychoral style favored by the Venetian school of the late Renaissance. The composer, the greatest German master of the late sixteenth and early seventeenth centuries, was a Protestant, but for a long time was in the musical service of the Catholic cathedral at Augsburg, and wrote music for both Catholic and Protestant use. The essence of the polychoral style is the alternate use of two (sometimes three or even more) distinct choruses called *cori spezzati* ("broken" choruses) when used this way. These choruses sing alternate passages in a freely antiphonal manner, or in an echo effect; they may join forces during sections of the piece, or reserve their combination for the conclusion, as they do in Hassler's motet. Occasional examples of choral music written in this manner have been traced back to the early fifteenth century, but the vogue for the polychoral style really begins with Willaert; he exploited it effectively because of the special arrangement of St. Mark's in Venice, which had separate lofts and organs in each of the cathedral apses. Willaert's successors at St. Mark's, Andrea and Giovanni Gabrieli, made far greater use of this style in their brilliant and colorful compositions, both vocal and instrumental, and Hassler had a first-hand acquaintance with the Venetian polychoral technique. As a youth of twenty he studied for a while with Andrea Gabrieli at Venice.

The present motet is one of two works for Pentecost from a collection of motets for the principal feasts of the whole ecclesiastical year, published in 1591. Hassler has used two four-part choruses of contrasting registers in this composition, the upper consisting of soprano, soprano, alto, alto, the lower of alto, tenor, tenor, bass. The two choruses join only in the last twelve bars of the piece, where there is real eight-part writing. There is a wonderful symmetry and balance to the over-all design of the piece. The opening and closing sections are the longest (bars 1–15, 58–69) and are strikingly different in texture from the rest of the piece and from each other. After the opening section, two phrases by the lower choir are answered by phrases in the upper choir. Then comes a middle section (bars 35–41) of a slightly different character, which is not answered; instead, the upper choir takes the lead (end of bar 41) and delivers two phrases which are answered by two phrases in the lower choir.

The end of each phrase is clearly articulated, in keeping with the prevalently chordal style; the first chord of every phrase is the same as the last chord of the previous phrase (even though the chord tones may be differently arranged) and is always an octave above or below that chord. The tonal answer in the opening fugal section and the generally chordal and tonal character of the following sections are significant manifestations of the increasing tendency toward tonality. Short imitative embellishments occur in a few of the sections. The influence of the Gabrielis is apparent in several features of Hassler's motet: the introduction of triple meter in the final peroration, the simple and attractive harmony, the driving rhythm, and the sonority of the climax. The personal style of the composer is evident, however, in the attractive melodic lines, and the high degree of craftsmanship.

The polychoral style was used in various forms, both sacred and secular (for example, by Palestrina in Masses, and by Lassus in motets), but it was particularly effective in the setting of Psalms, the verses of which generally fall into two halves, each of which states the same idea in a different way; nothing could be more natural or appropriate than to set the two statements antiphonally for two separate choruses.

The text used by Hassler is the vivid One Hundred Fiftieth Psalm. The translation in the King James version follows:

1. Praise ye the Lord. Praise God in his sanctuary: praise him in the firmament of his power.
2. Praise him for his mighty acts: praise him according to his excellent greatness.
3. Praise him with the sound of the trumpet: praise him with the psaltery and harp.

4. Praise him with the timbrel and dance: praise him with stringed instruments and organs.
5. Praise him upon the loud cymbals: praise him upon the high sounding cymbals.
6. Let every thing that hath breath praise the Lord.
   Praise ye the Lord.

Source: *Cantiones Sacrae de festis praecipius totius anni, 4, 5, 6, 7, 8, & plurium vocum*, No. 44, Augsburg, 1591.
Modern edition: H. Gehrmann, *H. L. Hasslers Werke, Cantiones Sacrae*, Bd. I, *DdT*, Vol. 2, p. 141, Leipzig, 1894.

# 28. Hans Leo Hassler (1564–1612)

## Polychoral Motet, *Laudate Dominum*

lau - da - - - - te Do- mi - num in san -
- jus, in san - ctis e - jus, in san - - -
Do - mi-num in san - - ctis e - - -
da - - - te Do - mi - num in san - -
- ctis e - - - jus,
- - ctis e - - - jus,
jus, in san - ctis e - - jus,
ctis ___ e - - jus,
lau - da - te e - um
lau - da - te e - um
lau - da - te e - um
lau - da - te e - um

20
in fir - ma - men - to vir - tu - tis e - jus, vir -
in fir - ma - men - to vir - tu - tis e - - jus, vir - tu - tis
in fir - ma - men - to vir - tu - tis e - jus, vir - tu - -
in fir - ma - men - to vir - tu - tis e - jus, vir -
lau - da - te e - um in vir - tu - ti - bus
laù - da - te e - um in vir - tu - ti - bus_
lau - da - te e - um in vir - tu - ti - bus
lau - da - te e - um in vir - tu - ti - bus
tu - - tis e - jus,
e - - - - jus,
- - - tis e - jus,
tu - - - tis e - jus,

e jus, lau - da - te e - um
25
— e - jus, lau - da - te e - um, lau - da - te e -
e - - jus, lau - da - te e - um, lau - da - te e -
e - - jus, lau - da - te e -

se - cun - dum mul - - - ti - tu - di - nem
um, se - cun - dum mul - ti - tu - di - nem
um, se - cun - dum mul - ti - tu - di - nem ma -
um se - cun - dum mul - ti - tu - di - nem

ma - gni - tu - di - nis e - jus,
30
ma - gni - tu - di - nis e - jus,
- gni - tu - di - nis e - jus,
ma - gni - tu - di - nis e - jus,
lau - da - te e - um in
lau - da - te e - um in
lau - da - te e - um in
lau - da - te e - um in
lau - da - te e - um in so - no tu - bae,
lau - da - te e - um in so - no tu - bae,
lau - da - te e - um in so - no tu - bae,
lau - da - te e - um in so - no tu - bae,
so - no tu - bae, lau -
so - no tu - bae, lau -
so - no tu - bae, lau -
so - no tu - bae,

35
- da - - - te e - - um in psal- te - ri-
da - - - - te e - um in psal- te - ri -
da - - - te e - - um in psal- te - ri -
lau - da - - - - te e - um in psal- te - ri -
40
o et ci - tha - ra, in psal - te - ri - o et ci - - -
o et ci - tha - ra, in psal- te - ri - o et ci tha - ra,
o et ci - tha - ra, in psal- te - ri - o et ci - - -
o et ci - tha - ra, in psal- te - ri - o et ci - - -

lau - da - te e - um in tym- pa - no et cho - ro, lau-
lau - da - te e - um in tym- pa - no et cho - ro, lau-
lau - da - te e - um in tym- pa - no et cho - ro, lau-
lau - da - te e - um in tym- pa - no et cho - ro, lau-
- tha - ra,
- tha-ra,
- tha - ra,
da- te e - um in chor - dis et or - ga - no,
45
da- te e - um in chor - dis et or - ga - no,
da- te e - um in chor - dis et or - - ga - no,
da- te e - um in chor - dis et or - ga - no,
lau- da - te
lau- da - te
lau - da -
lau- da - te

50
e - um in chor - dis et or - ga - no,
e - um in chor - dis et or - - ga - no,
- - te e - - um in chor-dis et or - ga-no,
e - - um in chor - dis et or - - ga - no,
𝅗𝅥 = 𝅗𝅥.
lau - da - te e - um in cym - ba - lis be - ne son - an - ti - bus,
lau - da - te e - um in cym - ba - lis be - ne son - an - ti - bus,
lau - da - te e - um in cym - ba - lis be - ne son - an - ti - bus,
lau - da - te e - um in cym - ba - lis be - ne son - an - ti - bus,

55
lau - da - te e - um in cym - ba - lis ju - bi - la - ti - o -
lau - da - te e - um in cym - ba - lis ju - bi - la - ti - o -
lau - da - te e - um in cym - ba - lis ju - bi - la - ti - o -
lau - da - te e - um in cym - ba - lis ju - bi - la - ti - o -
Om - nis spi - ri - tus lau - det Do - mi - num, om - nis
60
Om - nis spi - ri - tus lau - det Do - mi - num, om - nis
Om - nis spi - ri - tus lau - det Do - mi - num, om - nis
Om - nis spi - ri - tus lau - det Do - mi - num, om - nis
nis. Om - nis spi - ri - tus lau - det Do - mi - num, om - nis
nis. Om - nis spi - ri - tus lau - det Do - mi - num, om - nis spi - ri -
nis. Om - nis spi - ri - tus lau - det Do - mi - num, om - nis
nis. Om - nis spi - ri - tus lau - det Do - mi - num, om - nis

spi - ri - tus lau - det Do - - mi - num, lau - det Do - mi-
spi - ri - tus lau - det Do-mi- num, lau - det Do - mi-
spi - ri - tus lau - det Do - - mi - num, lau - det Do - mi-
spi - ri - tus lau - det Do-mi- num, lau - det Do - mi-
spi - ri - tus lau - - det Do -mi- num, lau - det Do - mi-
tus lau - det Do - - mi - num, lau - det Do - mi -
spi - ri - tus lau - det Do- mi- num, lau - det Do - mi-
spi - ri - tus lau - det Do - mi- num, lau - det Do - mi-
num, om - nis spi - ri - tus lau - det Do- mi - num, om - nis
65
num, om - nis spi - ri- tus lau - det Do-mi - num, om - nis
num, om - nis spi - ri - tus lau - det Do-mi - num, om - nis
num, om - nis spi - ri- tus lau - det Do-mi -num, om - nis
num, om - nis spi - ri- tus lau - det Do- mi - num, om - nis
num, om - nis spi - ri- tus lau - det Do-mi- num, om - nis spi-ri -
num, om - nis spi - ri- tus lau - det Do-mi- num, om - nis
num, om - nis spi - ri- tus lau - det Do-mi- num, om - nis

spi - ri - tus lau - det Do - - mi - num, lau - det Do - mi -
spi - ri - tus lau - det Do - mi - num, lau - det Do - mi -
spi - ri - tus lau - det Do - - mi - num, lau - det Do - mi -
spi - ri - tus lau - det Do - mi - num, lau - det Do - mi -
spi - ri - tus lau - det Do - mi - num, lau - det Do - mi -
tus lau - det Do - - mi - num, lau - det Do - mi -
spi - ri - tus lau - det Do - mi - num, lau - det Do - mi -
spi - ri - tus lau - det Do - - mi - num, lau - det Do - mi -

num, lau - det Do - mi - num.
num.
num, lau - det Do - mi - num.
num, lau - det Do - mi - num.
num, lau - det Do - mi - num.
num.
num, lau - det Do - mi - num.
num, lau - det Do - mi - num.

# 29. Claudio Merulo

## *Toccata Quinta, Secondo Tuono*

Examples 29 and 30 illustrate the idiomatic style and the high degree of virtuosity characteristic of keyboard music in the late Renaissance, especially in the two principal centers where such music was cultivated —the Venetian school of organ composition and the English virginalist school. Merulo, an organist at St. Mark's for nearly thirty years, was one of a number of brilliant composer-performers who were associated with that cathedral. These men employed mainly the *toccata*, *ricercar*, *canzona* and *fantasia*. Of these genres, the freest in style was the toccata; unlike the other three, it derived not from vocal models such as the motet or chanson, but from a short organ piece of improvisational character called the *intonazione*, whose original, humble function was to supply the pitch to the choir before the performance of a vocal composition.

The toccata of Example 29 is one of a collection of nine by Merulo printed in 1597 at Rome; in 1604 this set was followed by a second collection of Merulo's toccatas. The two books together comprise nineteen toccatas; they were planned so that two toccatas in each tone (that is, mode) are included, except for the second mode, in which there are three toccatas, and modes nine and ten (that is, the Aeolian mode on A and its plagal—Hypoaeolian—mode on E), for which there is only one toccata each. Example 29 is the third toccata in the second mode, and the fifth toccata in the first book; hence it is called *Toccata Quinta, Secondo Tuono*. The presence of the key signature indicates that it is a transposed mode, and therefore has its final on G, a fifth lower than the final of the untransposed second (or Hypodorian) mode. The practice of writing pieces in each of the modes is an instrumental parallel to composing vocal series in the modes—*cf.* Morales' *Magnificats* written for each mode, discussed in the commentary to Example 23—and is a modal prototype of Bach's plan of using all the keys in his *Well-tempered Clavier.*

The style of Merulo's toccatas is directly derived from such works as the *Intonazione* of Andrea Gabrieli, in which, within the course of some twelve or more bars, the composer begins with a few sustained chords, then turns to figuration, mostly rapidly-moving scale passages broken occasionally with trill- and turn-like figures, and ends with an ornamental cadence. (See the examples of *intonazioni* in Einstein, *Short History of Music,* No. 21, and *HAM,* No. 135.) Some of these *intonazioni* are expanded by a section in the middle in which the meandering flow of figuration changes briefly to the imitative style of the ricercar; then the piece returns to the freely improvisatory style of the first section.

This is the plan of Merulo's *Toccata Quinta.* The opening section of 28 bars has as its underlying framework a succession of chords which change at every bar or half-bar—occasionally at every two bars—around which is woven, in alternating hands, a rapidly moving line whose contour is predominantly one of ascending and descending scales sometimes broken by short decorative figures. Whenever a slight cadencing is suggested by the harmony, embellishing cadence-figures are used in the figuration, as at measures 7, 13, and 23, and elsewhere. Merulo makes little use of sequential figures, although these are not entirely absent (*e.g.,* bar 25). At bar 29 there is a complete change of texture to a ricercar-like section of ten bars, in which the subject introduced appears imitatively five more times; whenever it appears in the dominant it occurs as a tonal answer. After an ornamental cadence the improvisational manner of the first section is resumed (bar 39); its flow is interrupted briefly at two places through the use of slower note-values (49–50 and 56–57). The second of these interruptions is the only arpeggiated cadence in the piece.

Some of the toccatas in Merulo's collection have two sections in ricercar style with an improvisatory section between them as well as at the beginning and end of the piece; these, of course, are five-section forms. (Examples of the extended form appear in *GMB,* No. 149, and *HAM,* No. 153.) The further development of the toccata was carried on by Frescobaldi and, more significantly, by the North German organists, culminating in the transcendental works of this character by J. S. Bach.

The rests in the score are those of the original edition. If strict part-writing were followed, further rests would be necessary in several places; but these have not been added so that a more faithful picture of the original score might be presented.

Source: Washington, Library of Congress, *Toccate d'intavolature d'organo di Claudio Merulo da Coreggio . . . Libro Primo*, printed at Rome by Simone Verovio, 1597.

## 29. Claudio Merulo (1533–1604)

*Toccata Quinta, Secondo Tuono*

15
20
25

30
35
40

45
50
55

60
65

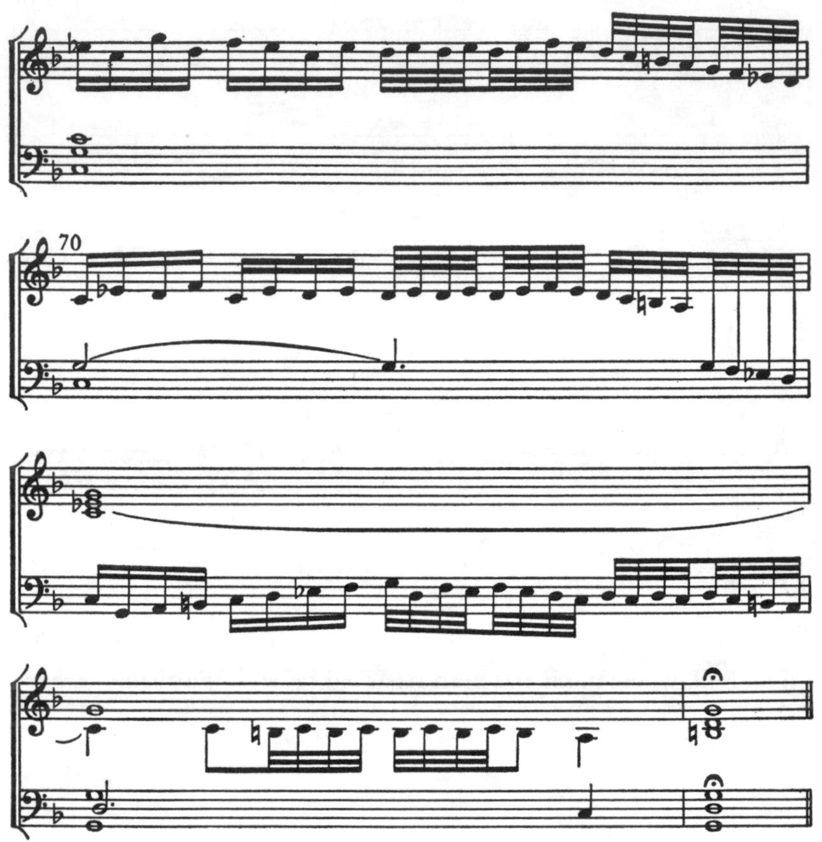
70

# 30. John Bull
## *Pavana* for the Virginal

The term *Virginalist*, applied to the English school of keyboard music of the late Renaissance, derives from the English form of harpsichord known as the *virginal* (often used in the plural: *virginals*). The virginalist repertory was of the greatest importance in the development of keyboard music; it was the earliest body of music written in a true harpsichord style, as distinct from organ style, based on a variety of technical figures that arose out of the nature of the instrument. Of the many excellent virginalists of Queen Elizabeth's time, no other was as brilliant as John Bull, whose music has been regarded rather unjustifiably as having been written primarily for the display of virtuosity. Although his virtuosity is strikingly apparent in Example 30, his other and more solid musical qualities are present in it as well.

The dance figured prominently among the various forms and styles used by the English composers; nearly half the compositions in the great Fitzwilliam Virginal Book are dances. The most favored among the dances was the *pavan*, a dance originating in Spain; the name is said to come from the Latin *pavo* ("peacock"), probably because of the dance's stately pace. The pavan became the traditional ceremonial court dance in the sixteenth century. It was sometimes paired with a succeeding galliard; but just as often it occurs as an individual piece. Except for the shorter pieces, little of the original dance character remains in the virginalist pavans because of the musical elaboration to which they are subjected. This example by Bull is from *Parthenia*, the first collection of virginal music to be printed in England (1611). It contains twenty-one pieces by the three leading English virginalists—Byrd, Bull, and Gibbons—five of which are pavans.

The piece has been reproduced here with its original barring, which sometimes marks off measures of two rather than of four half-notes. Because of this, the very symmetrical design of the composition is somewhat obscured. The form follows one customary way of writing a pavan: three different musical ideas are presented, each of which is followed immediately by a varied version of itself. The scheme is thus *A*, *A′*, *B*, *B′*, *C*, *C′*; each of the three large sections closes with a double bar. Each section in turn consists of two periods of two four-bar phrases each, if one counts by full bars and regards two half-bars as equal to one full bar. Following the bar numbers as they are marked in the score, however, the first phrase extends through bar 5 and is answered by the phrase in bars 6–10. Then follows the varied repetition of this section (11–25), which is exactly the length of the first half. The same plan and proportions are followed in the two subsequent sections.

The principal element of variation in the repeated sections is the addition of 16th-note figuration. The texture of these repeated sections is not unlike the Merulo toccata of Example 29, with its running figuration alternating in both hands and applied to a chordal background. However, the pavan is quite different in its stronger rhythmic pulse, sharper melodic definition, phrasing, and figural diversity. The tonal system is characteristically English in its attractive hovering between tonality and modality, its many cross-relations, its use of sequential passages, and its imaginative variety of figuration, which includes such unusual figures as those seen in bars 39 and 64–65. Bull apparently wished to make the degree of contrast between the first and second halves of each section a little more pronounced in each succeeding section. Since the prime factor of contrast is the 16th-note figuration, in each section the rapid movement decreases in the first half-section, and increases in the varied repetition of the second half, thus giving an effect of gradual climax to the whole.

The two oblique parallel strokes attached to a great many of the notes indicate that an ornamental figure is to be used on those notes; in many pieces another form is also found, consisting of only a single stroke. There is no contemporary explanation of the kind of ornament executed on these notes; it seems probable that the mordent and inverted mordent were the most frequently used, although undoubtedly other forms were used also. The existence of the same piece in various manuscripts with different ornamentation suggests that the use of such embellishments was probably left to the discretion of the player.

Source: *Parthenia, or the Maydenhead of the First Musicke that ever was printed for the Virginalls*, No. XII, London, 1611.

Modern edition: M. Glyn, *Twenty-one Old English Compositions . . . Parthenia*, London, 1927. The author's version of Bull's *Pavana* differs in some details from Miss Glyn's.

Facsimile edition: No. 3 of the Harrow Replicas, London, 1942.

## 30. John Bull (1563–1628)

### *Pavana* for the Virginal

25
30
35

40
45

50
55
60

65
70
75

# 31. Quodlibet: *Fricassée*

Example 31 is the first of four secular Renaissance compositions (Examples 31–34) from France, Germany, Italy, and England. Example 31, a sixteenth-century French piece in chanson style with the unlikely name of *fricassée* ("ragout"; *cf.* Spanish *ensalada,* "salad"), belongs to a general category of compositions known as *quodlibets* (Latin *quod,* "what" plus *libet,* "it will"), of which a number exist, and in which two or more well-known melodies are combined in some fashion. The most celebrated piece of this kind is the last variation of J. S. Bach's *Goldberg Variations,* which unites two popular tunes of his day. The quodlibet is a humorous piece. The essence of its humor lies in its heterogeneous juxtaposition of irrelevant melodies or phrases; in vocal quodlibets an extra element of humor is derived from the incongruous mixture of text as well as of music. Pieces of this character were especially popular in the sixteenth century, although the idea of the quodlibet is found in music of all periods, including the medieval.

This fricassée deserves its title; unlike most quodlibets, it employs not two or three complete tunes, but dozens of snippets from as many chansons. Thirty-nine of these chansons have been identified so far; many of them were written by such famous masters as Janequin, Josquin, Mouton, Sermisy, and Willaert. The name of the composer responsible for this remarkable composite piece is not known. In thirty of the identified chansons, he used only the incipit; in the other nine he used a part from the middle of a chanson; in every case he used the words as well as the melody of the fragment selected. He slightly modified some of the melodies to fit them into the musical context of the fricassée.

Because of the very special character of this composition it is difficult to make a satisfactory musical analysis; perhaps it is unnecessary, anyway. The outstanding feature of the piece is the astonishing skill with which the various borrowed motives have been woven together, and the grace and lightness with which they move. The fleetly-pacing rhythm and the delicate alternation of chordal and lightly polyphonic texture give the general effect of a chanson, but the piece lacks some of the traits usually associated with that style. For example, there are no real points of imitation, even though an imitative effect is cleverly suggested by the use of incipits of similar character, as at the very beginning; in a few cases, imitation in two voices occurs, as at measure 19 and measure 48. Also, unlike most chansons, the music is continuous, with no repetition of previous sections; sectionality, in fact, is avoided by means of overlapping cadences. The final cadence is made unusually attractive through its four-bar inverted pedal—that is, the note which is sustained in the soprano while the other voices proceed through changing harmonies.

A list of the chansons that have been identified in this quodlibet follows. Whenever an incipit is followed by a phrase in parentheses, the latter is the part of the chanson that has been used, rather than the incipit; otherwise the incipit is the part used.

Sermisy: *C'est a grant tort*
*C'est une dure departie*
*Dont vient cela*
*Tous mes amys*

Janequin: *Chansons, sonnons, trompettes*
*Petite, petite (Or sus, vous dormez trop)*
*Revirez vous (Resveillez vous)*
*Tout malostru (Or sus, vous dormez trop)*

Gombert: *Mort et fortune*

Heurteur: *Couvert de rose (Or my rendez)*

Nicolas: *Adieu soulas*

Josquin: *A l'ombre d'un buissonet (En l'ombre)*
*Baisez moy, ma doulce amye*
*Douleur me bat*
*Faulte d'argent*

Mouton: *Et pren ton ton (Prens ton con)*
*La, la, l'oysillon*

Lupi: *Changer non puis*
*Mon povre coeur*

Courtois: *Vire, vire Jehan*

Gascogne: *Mon povre coeur*

Passereau: *Ung peu plus haut*

Roquelay: *La my larrez (My larrez vous)*

Willaert: *Mon pere à fait faire un chasteau*

Chanson known, but composer unidentified:

*A la fontaine*
*A l'aventure (Povre coeur)*
*A l'aventure (Or suy-je pris)*
*Amy, souffrez que je vous ayme*
*Au monde recongnois (C'est donc par moy)*

*Boute luy ty mesme*
*C'est donc par moy*
*Et d'en bon jour*
*Et quand n'ay male (Quand j'ay beu du vin clairet)*
*Je m'en vois au vert boys*
*Je n'en puis plus*
*Le cueur est bon*
*Nous mangerons du rosty*
*Quand j'ai beu du vin clairet*
*Robin, comme l'entendez vous (A l'ombre d'un buissonet)*

Source: *Second livre contenant XXV chansons*, printed by P. Attaingnant, Paris, 1536.

Modern edition: F. Lesure, *Anthologie de la Chanson Parisienne au XVIe Siècle*, p. 19, Monaco, 1953. The identifications of the chansons were made by Isabelle Cazeaux, who collaborated in this edition.

# 31. Quodlibet: *Fricassée* (16th century)

suys ap - pel - lé - - e,
lard Il est grou-gnard, Hau Ma - ri - on m'a - - my -
es - per - du Vi - - re, vi - re Jehan, vi - re Jehan, Jehan-
lé - e suys ap - pel - lé - - e, Je n'en
Hau Ma - ri - on, Ma - ri - on. C'est
- - - e, Quant j'ay beu du vin clai - ret,
net - - te, Vi - gnon, vi - gnon, vi
puis plus, C'est u - ne du - re de -
u - ne du - re de - par - - ti - - e, Faul -
C'est donc par moy, Re - -
gnon, vi - gnet - te, qui te plan - ta il
par - ty - - - - e, De mon a -
te d'ar-gent c'est dou - leur non pa - - reil - - le Quant j'ay
vi - rez vous Cou - vert de rose et de mu - guet, Vi-
fut preud-hom' Chan - - ger ne puis, A l'a - ven -
my Ro - bin, Mon pere a faict faire ung chas - teau, gay-ment ma mi-
beu du vin clai - ret tout tour - ne, C'est sim - ple - ment don-
gnon, vi - gnon, vi - gnon, vi - gnet - - - te
tu - re, mon pau - vre cuer, he - las, qui nuyct et jour sous-
gnon - ne, A - dieu sou - las, La my lar - rez,

né con - gé a son a - my, Ung peu plus hau ung peu plus bas,
qui te plan - ta il fut preud - - - hom' Re - -
pi - - - - re, Il est ja - loux et a - mou -
Je m'en vais au vert boys, Nous man - ge - - rons du ros -
Nous man - ge - rons de ros - ty par - a - ven, -
so - - lu suis, Le cuer est bon, Pe - - ti - te, pe -
reux, A quoy tient il, a quoy tient il, dont vient
ti par a - ven - tu - re, s'il est cuist, Pe - ti - te, pe -
par a - ven - tu - re, A - my souf - frez que je vous
ti - te, Pour-quoy al - lez vous seul - let - - te, seul - -
ce - - la, Et d'en bon jour Est
ti - te, La, la, la, La, la,
ay - - - me,
let - - te, Hau Ma - ri - on m'a - - my - - -
ce bien faict, Ne suis je
la, Qui ne l'ay - - me -
A la fon - tai - ne du pré, Bou - te luy ty mes - me
- - e, A - dieu le frè - re voy - la l'huys,
pas bien mal - heu - reux, Je m'en vois au
roit, Et qu'en n'ay ma - le ny de - nier, je n'en boy

de la clain- que main jour - dain, Cu - ré ve - nez en
Lais - se my faire, he - las Et
vert boys, Pren ton ton, Et vi - re, vi - re
point, je n'en boy point, Bai - sez moy ma doulce a -
nos mai - sons, Vi - - re, vi - re Jehan, Ro - bin com-
pren ton ton. Hé - las my lar - rez
Jehan, vi - re Jehan, Ja - non, A l'om - bre d'ung buys - son -
my - - e, Je suis sai - si du laz d'a - -
me l'en - ten - dez vous, hau Ma - ri - on m'a - my - -
vous ain - si, La, la, la, A l'om-
net, Pour vous ay - mer, pour vous ay - -
mors, Ro - bin, com - me l'en - ten - dez vous,
e.
bre d'ung buys - son - net, C'est par trop dict.
mer, Chan - tons, son - nons, trom - pet - - tes, Dou - leur me bat.
Chan - tons, son - nons, trom - pet - - tes, Chan - tons, son - nons, trom - pettes.

# 32. Ludwig Senfl

## Lied, *Oho, So Geb' Der Mann Ein'n Pfenning*

The piece by Ludwig Senfl, Example 32, is a characteristic and attractive illustration of the polyphonic German Lied. Many *Lieder* were composed and published in Germany in the sixteenth century. This particular Lied comes from a collection of 115 compositions printed in 1544 by Johann Ott; the collection includes *Lieder* by other composers of German songs—Isaac, Mahu, von Bruck, and Dietrich—as well as works with texts in languages other than German by Crequillon, Gombert, and Verdelot. The German polyphonic Lied was one of the distinct national secular forms of the Renaissance, corresponding in its national character to the Spanish villancico, the French chanson, and the later Italian madrigal and English madrigal and lute song.

A peculiarity of the polyphonic Lied is that a German folksong is often used as a cantus firmus. Senfl, in common with other Lied composers, treated these songs in various ways in his settings: sometimes he writes in a predominantly chordal style, with occasional passages in which the voices are allowed a slight rhythmic independence; sometimes he treats the folktune as a canon between two voices while the other voices are in free counterpoint; and sometimes (as in Example 32) he uses the folktune as a long-note cantus firmus around which he weaves a light-textured polyphonic fabric whose motives are derived from the phrases of the tune. In each of these styles the original melody is almost always given to the tenor voice, which in many settings is the only voice underlaid with a text. Most of the Lied settings are in four voices, although several are in five, and some in six.

The texts used by Senfl cover a wide variety of subjects: earthy approaches to love, the hunt, drinking (like this one), ballad-like narrations; more elegant texts, obviously intended for Senfl's court audience, extoll loyalty, good breeding, and such traits; other texts are sentimental expressions of grief at departure from a loved one or at the faithlessness of a lover.

In this drinking song, the original folk melody does not appear until measure 20 (in the tenor), where it is treated in notes of twice the value of those that predominate in the other voices. The imitative counterpoint of the other parts is derived almost entirely from this tune, beginning with the opening duet. This manner of treating a cantus firmus is usually referred to as "anticipating" imitation (German, *Vorimitation*), and is very frequently employed by German composers right through to the period of J. S. Bach. The piece has many fine touches of craftsmanship—for instance, the use of the (melodic) interval of the fifth at many places apart from its position as the opening interval of the melody and the contrapuntal figures derived therefrom; it is given a final emphatic statement by the bass in the last two bars. The fifth is also used harmonically as an inner pedal in the tenor for the last five bars of the piece against changing harmonies in the other parts. Another interesting detail is the chain of sequences in the bass from the end of bar 15 through bar 19, stemming from a figure that had occurred previously in the soprano in bars 11, 13, and 14.

Some of Senfl's *Lieder* have extra verses which are appended at the end of the music, and are intended to be performed strophically. Example 32 has only the single couplet, which is underlaid in all voices in the original print, and which may be translated thus:

Oho, if the man would give some money
Then we could have more wine.

This Lied also appeared in another collection of polyphonic folk songs printed in 1544 by Wolfgang Schmeltzel, with some variants of both text and music. The Schmeltzel version is as follows:

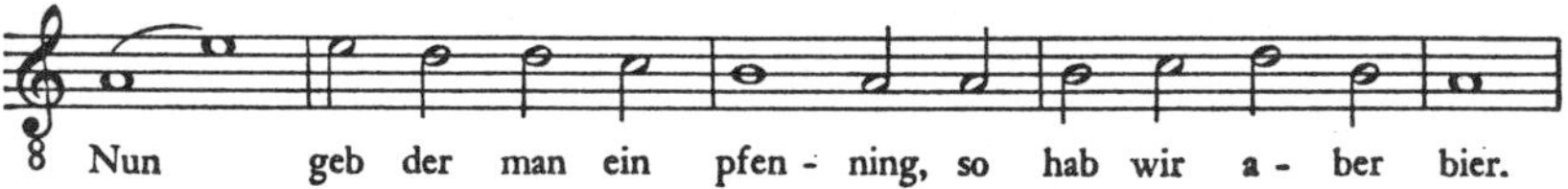


Source: J. Ott, *Hundert und funfftzehen guter newer Liedlein*, No. 21, Nürnberg, 1544.

Modern editions: R. Eitner, *Lieder mit deutschem, lateinischem, französischem, und italienischem Text zu vier, fünf, und sechs Stimmen*, Vol. I, p. 60, Berlin, 1876. A. Geering and W. Altweg, *Ludwig Senfl, sämtliche Werke*, Vol. V, p. 38. Basel, 1949.

## 32. Ludwig Senfl (*ca.* 1490–1556)

## Lied, *Oho, so geb' der Mann ein'n Pfenning*

a - ber Wein, a - ber Wein, so geb' der Mann
ho, so geb' der Mann
ho, so geb' der Mann ein'n
Wein, so hab' wir a - ber
ein'n Pfen - - - - ning, ein'n Pfen - ning,
ein'n Pfen - - - - ning, so hab' wir
Pfen - ning, so hab' wir
Wein, Wein, so hab'
so hab' wir a - ber Wein, a - ber Wein, a - ber
a - ber Wein,
a - ber Wein, o - ho
wir a - ber Wein, o - ho,
Wein, o - ho, so geb' der,
o - - - - ho, so geb' der Mann ein'n
so geb' der Mann ein'n Pfen - ning, so hab' wir a - ber
so geb' der Mann ein'n Pfen - ning, so
Mann ein'n Pfen - - - ning, so hab' wir a - ber Wein.
Pfen - ning, so hab' wir a - - ber Wein.
Wein .
hab' wir a - ber Wein, a - ber Wein.

# 33. Carlo Gesualdo
# Madrigal, *Moro lasso*

The madrigal *Moro lasso* by Carlo Gesualdo is the composition of a daring experimenter whose most characteristic work came at the end of the great period of the Italian madrigal. The age in which he lived was a revolutionary one in the history of music; but none of his contemporaries, not even Monteverdi, approached the harmonic audacity of such works as this one from his Sixth Book of Madrigals, first printed in 1611. Gesualdo's earliest madrigals show a mastery of the technique but give no hint of the extraordinary style he developed in his later compositions, all of which are featured by passages of extreme chromaticism and by a freedom of modulation that often has a strangely modern ring.

Gesualdo had a definite predilection for short texts, especially those dealing with pain, sorrow, or death; he tried to project their moods with the utmost directness of expression. He rarely engages in word-painting, but depends on the highly charged atmosphere of his music to vivify the mood of the words. His general procedure is to alternate chordal passages of extreme chromatic harmony with passages of strict imitation; sometimes he combines the two methods of writing.

The design of *Moro lasso* is ingeniously adapted to the poem, which consists of three short stanzas, the first two of which are identical except for the last word in each stanza. For his setting Gesualdo has used an *A*, *A*, *B* plan, similar to that of the troubadour canso, the Meistergesang, and the Ars Nova ballade (Examples 6, 22, and 17). There is a difference between the first and second *A* sections of this madrigal, however, in that the second section (which begins at bar 23), although it uses the same musical material as the first and has the same length, begins its various subsections at different pitches; also, the voices are rearranged, and there are some slight rythmical differences. The last section (which begins at bar 45) is completely different.

The haunting opening phrase drifts in a short course of six bars through chords from C♯ major to A minor, and is overlapped by the beginning of the next phrase in the soprano. The second phrase (bars 6–13) is written in strict contrapuntal style, the voices entering by pairs (except the last entry) in close imitation, and without chromaticism. The third phrase (bars 13–19) begins imitatively and in chromatically shifting harmony with two motives, one ascending (altos I and II), the other descending (soprano, tenor, and bass); then, after a simultaneous *sospiro* (Italian, "sigh," also "pause") in all voices, changes to chordal texture. The last bars of this phrase (17–19) are then repeated verbatim, in the manner of an echo.

The close parallelism of music and text in the two *A* sections has already been mentioned above. The *B* section begins with a short imitative phrase on "O dolorosa forte" that proceeds innocently enough until its surprising turn at the cadence chord (bar 48). This phrase is then repeated immediately in a different voice arrangement, with the principal melody (soprano) a third higher, although harmonically the phrase has shifted to the fifth above. This phrase is answered by a short homophonic phrase on "chi dar vita mi puo" (bars 53–55). After this the text consists only of several repetitions of the phrase "ahi, mi da morte," which is set by Gesualdo imitatively and with two motives; one of these is conjunct and partially chromatic (it appears first in the soprano, second half of bar 55), the other has an initial drop of a fifth which turns back on itself, sometimes by a leap, sometimes by a chromatic step (it appears first in the tenor, bar 56). In this final section, the first of these motives is kept in the two upper voices, the second motive in the two lower voices, while the middle voice has them both.

The highly personal character of this work and its tortured expression of despair are produced mainly by the use of chromaticism in both harmony and melody, and by passing dissonances, cross-relations, and sudden major-minor changes of harmony in which the piece abounds. Gesualdo had no followers, and his style has been aptly called "a fascinating bypath in the history of music"; but there is an undeniable in-

## 33. Carlo Gesualdo (*ca.* 1560–1613)

### Madrigal, *Moro lasso*

tensity to his music, and there is no question about the great skill with which it is written.

The translation of the poem:

I die, alas! from my pain,
And who can give me life,
Alas, kills me and will not give me life.

I die, alas! from my pain,
And who can give me life,
Alas, kills me and will not give me succour.

Oh painful lot,
Who can give me life,
Alas, gives me death.

Source: *Madrigali a Cinque Voci Libro Sesto.* Printed by Gio. Jac. Carlino, Gesualdo, 1611. 23 madrigals.

Modern edition: W. Weismann, ed., *8 Madrigale für fünfstimmigen Chor,* Leipzig, 1931.

ahi, che m'an - ci - de e non vuol
15
ahi, che m'an - ci - de e non vuol
ahi, che m'an - ci - - - de e non vuol
ta, ahi, che m'an - ci - de e non
ahi, che m'an - ci - de e non vuol
dar - mi vi - - ta, e non vuol dar- mi vi - - ta.
20
dar - mi vi - - ta, e non vuol dar- mi vi - - ta.
dar - mi vi - ta, e non vuol dar - mi vi - ta.
vuol dar - mi vi - ta, e non vuol dar - mi vi - ta.
dar - mi vi - ta, e non vuol dar - mi vi - ta.
Mo - - ro las - so al mio duo - lo,
25
Mo - - ro las - so al mio duo - - lo,
Mo - - ro las - so al mio duo - - lo, e chi mi
Mo - - ro las - so al mio duo - lo, e
e chi

e chi mi può dar vi - - - -
30
e chi mi può dar vi - - - - - - ta,
può dar vi - - - - ta, e chi mi
chi mi può dar vi - - - - ta, e
mi può dar vi - - ta, e chi
- ta, e chi mi può dar vi - - - - ta,
e chi mi può dar vi - - - - - ta,
può dar vi - - - - - ta,
chi mi può dar vi - - - - - ta,
mi può dar vi - - - - - - - ta,
35
Ahi, che m'an- ci - de e non vuol
Ahi, che m'an-ci - de e non vuol
ahi, che m'an - ci - - - de e non vuol
Ahi, che m'an - ci - de e non vuol
Ahi, che m'an - ci - - de e non vuol

dar mi ai - ta, e non vuol dar mi ai - ta.
dar mi ai - ta, e non vuol dar mi ai - ta.
dar mi ai - ta, e non vuol dar mi ai - ta.
dar mi ai - - - ta, e non vuol dar mi ai - - ta.
dar mi ai - ta, e non vuol dar mi ai - ta.
O
O dolo - ro - sa for - te,
O dolo - ro - sa for - te, O
O dolo - ro - sa for - te, O dolo -
O dolo - ro - - sa for - - te,
dolo - ro - sa for - te, chi dar vi - - ta mi
O dolo - ro - sa for - te, chi dar vi - - ta mi
dolo - ro - sa for - te, chi dar vi - - ta mi
ro - - sa for - - te, chi dar vi - - ta mi
chi dar vi - - ta mi

può, ahi, mi da mor - te,
55
può, ahi, mi da mor - te, ahi,
può, ahi, mi da mor - te,
può, ahi, mi da mor - - te, ahi,
può, ahi,
ahi, mi da mor - - te,
60
mi da mor - te, ahi, mi da mor -
ahi, mi da mor - te, ahi, mi da
mi da mor - - te, ahi, mi da
mi da mor - te,
ahi, ahi, mi da mor - te.
65
te, ahi, mi da mor - - - - te.
mor - te, ahi, mi da mor - - - - te.
mor - te, ahi, mi da mor - te.
ahi, mi da mor - - - - te.

# 34. John Dowland

## Lute Ayre, *My Thoughts Are Wing'd With Hope*

The first examples of published lute music of the early sixteenth century included transcriptions of polyphonic vocal music like the piece offered as Example 21 of this book. In the middle and late sixteenth century many Italian, French, and German transcriptions of part music were printed as vocal solos with lute accompaniments consisting of an arrangement for the lute of the lower parts of the original choral piece. In a way this was only a written acknowledgment of an ancient practice whereby one part of a polyphonic piece was sung while the other parts were assigned to instruments. English collections of pieces like this—called *lute songs* or *lute ayres*—began to be published in 1597 (Example 34 is from the first of these collections), and enjoyed wide popularity both at home and abroad during the first quarter of the seventeenth century. In fact, the ayre began to replace the madrigal in English favor, and relatively few books of English madrigals were published after the vogue of the ayre was established.

The English lute song books were distinguished from those of other countries by the fact that they contained both polyphonic and accompanied-solo versions of the same ayre. The versions were printed on two facing pages of a book, as shown in Fig. 1, so that if an ensemble performance were desired, all performers could read their parts from the one book. Thus three distinct kinds of performance were possible: a solo with lute accompaniment, a solo song with the other parts played by melody instruments such as viols, and an *a cappella* vocal polyphonic piece. The titles of lute books usually indicate this (see *Source* listing at end of this commentary).

The tender and playful love song, *My Thoughts*, is a characteristic ayre by the most eminent of the English lutenist-composers. It is strophic, and has an appealing melody which moves in a succession of regular phrases in which the rhythmical pattern set up in the first phrase is repeated throughout, with slight inflections of rhythm in most phrases.

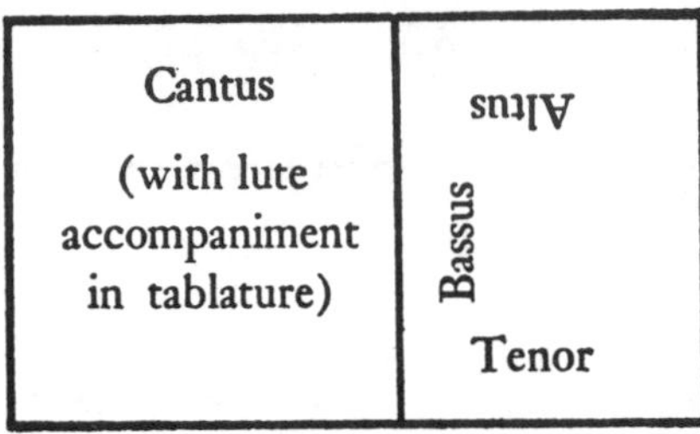


Fig. 1

The phrases are clearly cadenced in the tonic and dominant, and in one case (bar 12) in the relative major. While tonality has been more or less present in several of the previous compositions in this book, this is the first in which it is so clearly established. There is no repetition or recurrence of melody, but all phrases have a natural melodic affinity. *My Thoughts* was also set by Dowland as an instrumental piece in his *Lachrimae, or Seaven Teares Figured in Seaven Passionate Pavans. . . set forth for the Lute, Viols, or Violins. . .* (1604), and it also appears elsewhere as a lute solo.

The lute accompaniment of *My Thoughts* is a fairly close approximation of the three lower parts of the four-part choral setting, but arranged with the traditional freedom of the lute to add or drop voices according to the exigencies of the instrument and the musical situation of the movement. The transcription is not literal, like the one in Example 21, but carries out the implied part-writing by lengthening certain notes. The bass, which may have been reinforced by a bass viol in actual performance, has some rhythmic and melodic independence; the suggestion of *hemiola* rhythm—alteration of 3/4 and 6/8 meter—at certain cadences results from the typical lute broken-chord cadence formula, and should be considered in relation to the upper parts.

The original edition prints the following two additional verses. It will be noted that the last words of lines one and three of the second verse ("carry," "vary") have one more syllable than the words at the corresponding places in the first and third verses, so that the note in the melody at this place must be repeated.

2. And you my thoughts that some mistrust do carry,
 If for mistrust my mistress do you blame,
 Say though you alter, yet you do not vary,
 As she doth change, and yet remain the same:
  Distrust doth enter hearts, but not infect,
  And love is sweetest seasoned with suspect.

3. If she for this, with clouds do mask her eyes,
 And make the heavens dark with her disdain,
 With windy sighs disperse them in the skies,
 Or with thy tears dissolve them into rain,
  Thoughts, hopes, and love return no more
  Till Cynthia shine as she hath done before.

Source: *The First Booke of Songes or Ayres of foure partes with Tableture for the Lute: So made that all the partes together, or either of them severally may be song to the Lute, Orpherian or Viol da gambo,* No. 3, London, 1597. (The Orpherion was similar to a guitar, with wire strings.)

Modern edition: E. Fellowes, T. Dart, and N. Fortune, *John Dowland, Ayres for Four Voices, MB,* Vol. VI, p. 4, London, 1953. The frontispiece of this volume is a facsimile of *My Thoughts* from the original print of 1597.

## 34. John Dowland (1563–1626)

## Lute Ayre, *My Thoughts Are Wing'd With Hope*

5
10
My thoughts are wing'd with hopes, my hopes with love,
mount love, un - to the moon— in clear - est night,
And say as she doth in the hea - vens move,

15
in earth so wanes and wax - eth my de - light,
20
And whis - per this but soft - ly in her __ ears,
hope oft doth hang the head, and trust ___ shed tears.

# 35. *Passamezzo d'Italie*

This example and the one following are compositions written for instrumental ensemble, a medium that became increasingly popular as the Renaissance drew to a close. Example 35 is from the large repertory of sixteenth-century dance music; it was written at a time when the dance was becoming stylized into an important art form.

*Passamezzos* were composed in great numbers in the late sixteenth and early seventeenth centuries. The origins and actual meaning of the name are uncertain. The word is a shortened form of *passo e mezzo* (Italian, "step-and-a-half"), and may refer to steps used in the dance or to music in halved note values; several other derivations have also been suggested. The tempo and character of the passamezzo are those of a livelier pavane (see Example 30), a form which the passamezzo replaced about the middle of the sixteenth century. Passamezzos exist in many lute and keyboard settings, as well as in versions for instrumental ensemble.

The passamezzo was essentially a set of variations on an ostinato bass; the bass itself was varied during its several repetitions, but its outline was always followed. Composers used one of two simple bass melodies in writing a passamezzo—one in a minor key called the *passamezzo antico*, the other in major called the *passamezzo moderno*. (See the antico bass at the end of this commentary.) In the successive variations not only the bass but the melody it accompanied was varied, the only unchanging factor being the series of underlying harmonies which prevailed in all variations. The musical structure thus engendered has been appropriately described as a variation on ostinato harmonies.

The *Passamezzo d'Italie* was published in 1583, and is a fine example of the form based on the antico bass. It is followed by a *Represa* (Italian, "recommencement") which is itself also a series of variations.

The reprise was not essential to the passamezzo, but was often added by composers.[1] Example 35 consists of a sixteen-bar unit which is repeated in a varied manner four times, each repetition being called a *modo* (Italian, "manner"). Since the opening section is itself a variation of a still simpler melody which does not appear in the music—this practice was usual in Renaissance variation forms—there are five modi in all. (The original melody is given at the end of this commentary.)

The over-all design of the passamezzo has an interesting symmetry. The first two modi form a pair; in both modi the musical material in the two most important parts (bass and upper voice) is similar, and the two modi are linked together at the cadence of the first by continued movement in the tenor part. Modi three and four also form a pair; in both the bass takes on lively rhythmical activity, and the upper voice is reduced in melodic range and rhythmical energy. Like the first pair, these modi are linked rhythmically at the cadence. The cadences at the end of modi two and four are definite, ending simultaneously in all parts. The fifth variation is a peroration which embraces the musical character of both the preceding pairs; the character of the first pair dominates its first half, while the second half uses elements found mainly in the second pair.

The reprise is taken up with no stop in the flow of rhythmical movement; in fact, the last bar of modo five is purposely omitted and a cadence avoided so that the end of the passamezzo passes directly into the beginning of the reprise. The three modi of the reprise are each eight bars long. A different musical design is used here, in which all three modi begin in the same way and then pursue different courses after the third measure. A new bass melody is employed in the reprise, derived from the bass movement in the third and fourth modi of the passamezzo; the melody appears to be a shortened version of the original tune. The whole character of the reprise is simpler than that of the passamezzo.

The occasional rather startling augmented sixth chords are definitely indicated in the original score. They are primarily the result of melodic movement in bass and soprano in which the up-and-down movement

[1] In the book from which this dance comes, the passamezzo and reprise are followed by a *Saltarello* and *Represa*. The saltarello uses the antico bass and is in triple meter, so that passamezzo and saltarello together form a kind of large scale *Tanz und Nachtanz* (see *M of M*, No. 22).

of a whole step on certain degrees of the scale is changed to a half-step. The clearest instance is in measure 81; measure 23 is the same, with a melodic embellishment added in the soprano; measure 38 involves harmonic circumstances in the bass.

The passamezzo antico bass:

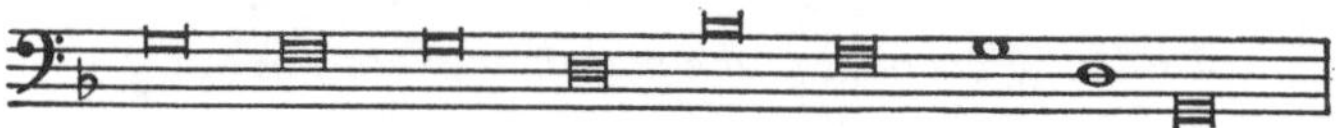

The original melody on which the *Passamezzo d'Italie* is based (from a dance in a publication of Phalèse, 1571):

Source: *Chorearum molliorum Collectanea*, printed by P. Phalèse, Antwerp, 1583.

Modern edition: F. Blume, *Studien zur Vorgeschichte der Orchestersuite im 15–16 Jahrhundert, Anhang B* (*Musikbeispiele*), p. 47, Leipzig, 1925.

## 35. *Passamezzo d'Italie* (16th century)

25
30
Terzo modo
35
40
45

Quarto modo
50
55
60
Quinto modo
65
70

75
Represa
80
85
Secondo modo
90
95

Terzo modo
100

# 36. Orlando Gibbons
## *In Nomine*

English compositions for instrumental ensemble were an important part of the instrumental music of the late sixteenth and early seventeenth centuries. We have from this repertory a very large number of fantasies and dances, and also a peculiarly English instrumental form called the *In Nomine*. About one hundred fifty In Nomines exist; some of them are set for keyboard or lute, but most call for an ensemble of instruments; in Elizabethan and Jacobean times this ensemble was usually a "consort of viols."

The general character of the In Nomine is similar to that of the *fantasia*—called the *fancy* in England: a motet-like instrumental piece which develops a succession of themes in imitative style, like the ricercar. (Morley aptly described the fancy thus: "when a musician taketh a point at his pleasure, and wresteth and turneth it as he list. . . ." *Plaine and Easie Introduction*, 1597). The In Nomine has a special and indispensable factor that distinguishes it from the fancy, however: a long-note cantus firmus which is always present as one of its parts. The cantus firmus used for all pieces called In Nomine is the melody of the Antiphon for Second Vespers of Trinity Sunday. (The melody is printed at the end of this commentary.) Since the words "in nomine" do not occur anywhere in the text of this antiphon, the name of the form remained a puzzle until shortly over a decade ago, when Gustave Reese showed that it comes from a Mass by Taverner (*Missa Gloria Tibi Trinitas*) which uses the antiphon melody as a cantus firmus throughout the Mass, including the text of the Benedictus ("Benedictus qui venit *in nomine Domini*"), the last three words of which are set to the whole cantus firmus. Taverner himself made an instrumental transcription of this part of the Benedictus, calling it "In Nomine" after the words with which the cantus firmus melody begins in this section of his Mass; other composers did likewise, thus starting what came to be a whole new species of composition.[1]

The unique manuscript source from which Example 36 comes is not dated, but it must have been written during the first quarter of the seventeenth century. In this piece the cantus appears in its usual position as the second part from the top (alto viol). In some In Nomines composers added rhythmical and melodic embellishments to the tune, but Gibbons presents it in simple and straightforward fashion, with two very slight rhythmical inflections (bars 8 and 41). The other voices proceed in the manner of a fantasia, taking up five different subjects in turn, and treating each as a point of imitation. None of the subjects is related to the cantus, with the possible exception of the rising third at the beginning of the first subject, which may be related to the beginning of the cantus. The imitative entries of the first subject are rather widely spaced, but at the beginning of the second subject (bar 16, treble viol) the entries are in close imitation. There is a return of the first subject at bar 23. At bar 30 a third subject enters (treble viol), and a fourth at bar 36 (tenor viol), again in close imitation. The final entry is at bar 43 (bass viol), and in this section the fourth subject also recurs. The counterpoint is modal, although the modality is softened from time to time by the modification of scale degrees. The piece as a whole possesses that inimitable combination of sombreness and inner glow characteristic of much English music of the late Renaissance.

The antiphon *Gloria tibi Trinitas* as it appears in the *LU*, p. 914:

Glo- ri- a ti- bi Tri- ni- tas ae- qua- lis, u- na De- i- tas,
et an- te om- ni- a sae- cu- la, et nunc, et in

per- pe- tu- um.

[1] See the beginning of the In Nomine passage of Taverner's Mass in G. Reese, *MR*, p. 780; also, Reese, "The Origins of the English *In Nomine*," *JAMS*, Spring, 1949, p. 7.

The cantus firmus used in the In Nomine varies in a few details from this *LU* version because English composers used the slightly different version in the Sarum Antiphonary.

Source: Oxford, Bodleian Library MSSD. 212–16.
Modern edition: The version in this present volume is reprinted from *MB*, Vol. IX, p. 42, *Jacobean Consort Music*, ed. by T. Dart and W. Coates, © 1955, with the permission of the Royal Musical Association, and Stainer & Bell, Ltd.

## 36. Orlando Gibbons (1583–1625)

*In Nomine*

25
30
35
40
45

50
55

# 37. Emilio de' Cavalieri
## Scene from *Rappresentatione di Anima e di Corpo*

Example 37 is the first composition in this book of the Baroque era. Although its composer, Cavalieri, lived somewhat earlier than the composers of the immediately preceding examples, he represents a spirit and style much more oriented toward the future than theirs. He was one of the leading members of the *Camerata* of Florence, a group whose efforts to recapture what they conceived to be the style of the ancient Greeks in the presentation of drama led to the great Baroque form of the opera. The first fruit of the Florentine experiments was the accompanied monody—the expressive declamation called the *stile rappresentativo*—in which most of the early operas were set; Cavalieri's *Rappresentatione* is the earliest printed work in which this monody occurs.[1] The scene included in Example 37 begins with a characteristic monody which resumes after a short trio and shorter ritornello. Underneath the bass line, and continuing throughout, is the continuo (usually, as here, a figured bass), a feature peculiar to all concerted music of the Baroque period.

Cavalieri's *Rappresentatione* has been called the first oratorio; but it is not in the direct line of development of the oratorio as such, and is more properly considered as the earliest example of the special category of the sacred opera. It has many features that were never part of the oratorio—such as dances—and directions are given in its Foreword for action, staging, and costumes. Its close connection with the oratorio, however, is made obvious by the fact that its first performance (Rome, 1600) was at the *Congregazione dell'Oratorio*, the "place of prayer,"

[1] Caccini's monodies in *Le nuove musiche* were printed in 1601. Peri, in his Foreword to *Euridice* (1601), says that "Cavalieri, before any other of whom I know, enabled us with marvelous invention to hear our kind of music upon the stage."

which later gave its name to the oratorio as a musical form. The libretto of the *Rappresentatione* may be described as a morality play with allegorical characters—Pleasure, Prudence, the Intellect, the World; choral groups portray the Damned Souls in Hell, and the Blessed Souls in Heaven. The two principal characters are the Soul and the Body, and the moral tone of the scene of Example 37 is typical of the whole piece: the Soul impresses upon the Body the necessity of avoiding the deceitful pleasures of the world if salvation, with its priceless gift of eternal life, is to be achieved. This particular scene occurs near the middle of Act II of the three-act opera.

Example 37 begins immediately after a trio in which Pleasure and her two companions have sung an enticing invitation to the Body to enjoy the earthly delights they promise him. Then (bars 1–21) the Soul sternly rebukes them and bids them depart; they leave singing their intention of finding other victims (bars 22–44), and the Body then questions the wisdom of foregoing such pleasures (bars 45–51). The Soul calls upon Heaven to answer these questions (bars 52–59) in an outstanding passage in which Cavalieri exploits the device of the echo with extraordinary effectiveness and imagination (bars 60–81). The echo repeats the end of each question asked, but each echo turns out to be an actual, wise answer to the question. The musical echo was used occasionally throughout the sixteenth century, but in the Baroque period it appears in so many compositions, both vocal and instrumental, that it may well be considered a definite feature of Baroque style.

In general, Cavalieri's monody is not as expressive as that of some of the other composers who employed the *stile rappresentativo* (see the examples by Caccini and Monteverdi in *M of M*, Nos. 30 and 31), and often tends to take on a definite rhythmic and melodic contour which the others purposely avoided; one such passage is seen in bars 52–59. Unlike the other early operas, the *Rappresentatione* has numerous choruses, all in simple chordal style similar to the opening of the trio in bar 21. Cavalieri's figures under the bass represent the actual distance above the bass of the interval demanded, unlike later practice in which the octave register is disregarded. (In this and the subsequent examples in this book with a figured bass, the editor's realization is in smaller notes than those that occur in the printed score.) The sharp sign is used for the major third, even when this means raising a flat to a natural.

The breath marks indicated by commas are in the original print, where the sign used is an *S* (for *sospiro*).

The translation of the text:

*Anima*

Away, away, false sirens full of fraud and deceit; lamentation always attends the end of your song. Every delight is brief, but that which will bring torment should not end.

*Pleasure and Her Companions*

Then since this happy company does not please you,
We shall go through the way where others desire us,
Who, to be happy, will gaze upon us by the hundreds.

*Corpo*

I know not if it were good to leave such pleasure, which the world so prizes.

*Anima*

I shall ask it of Heaven, which never hides the truth. Let us see what it answers.
Does the wise man love earthly pleasure or flee it? *Flee it.*
What is it, that man seeks it, and seeks in vain? *Vain.*
What gives death to the soul through displeasure?—*pleasure.*
How does he who desires life gain life—*he loves* [. . . brama. -*ama.*]
Does he love the beauties of the world, or God? *God.*
Then he will die who desires pleasure, is it true? *True.*
Now that which heaven has told you, behold I state in sum: flee vain pleasure, love the true God.

Source: *Rappresentatione di anima, et di corpo, Nuovamente posta in Musica dal Sig. Emilio del Cavalliere, per recitar Cantando*, Rome, 1600. Facsimile edition, Rome, 1912.

Modern edition: G. Tebaldini, *Rappresentatione di anima . . .*, Turin, 1914(?).

## 37. Emilio de' Cavalieri (*ca.* 1550–1602)

### Scene from *Rappresentatione di anima e di corpo*

Anima
Via, via, fal - se Si-re - ne, di fro - di e in-gan - ni
pie - ne; Il fin del vo - stro can - to oc - cu-pa -sem - pr'il
pian - to. O - gni di - let - to è bre - ve, ma quel ch'af-
flig - ge- ra fi - nir non de - ve.

Piacere, e compagni
Hor poi che non viag-gra - da Sa lie - ta com - pa - gni - a,
Ce n'an- de - rem per stra - da,
Ce n'an - de- rem per stra - da, Dov' al - tri ci de -
Ce n'an - de- rem per stra - da, Dov'
Do - - ve al - tri ci de - si - a:
si - a, Dov' al - tri ci de - si - a: Che
al - tri ci de - si - - - a: Che per ha -
Che per ha- ver con - ten - to, Ver - ran- no a
per ha - ver con - ten - to. Ver - - ran - no a cen- to a
ver con- ten - to. Ver - - ran- no a cen- to a cen - - -
cen - to a cen - to, Che per ha- ver con -
cen - - - - to. Che per ha - ver con- ten - to,
- - - to. Che per ha - ver con-ten - to, Ver -

ten - - to, Ver - ran-no a cen-to a cen - - to. Ritornello
Ver - - ran-no a cen-to a cen- - to.
ran-no a cen-to a cen - - - - - to.
6 ♯6 ♯11 ♯ 13 4
40
11 6 6 4 ♯
Corpo
45
Non so s'e sta-to be - ne La- sciar tan- to pia- cer, che'l
6 7 10
Anima
50
mon- do tie - ne. Vo di - man - dar- ne al Cie -
4 7 4 ♯3 6 4 4 ♯

55
lo, Ch'il ver mai non a - scon - de, Ve - diam quel
60
che ri-spon - de. A - ma il mon-dan pia - cer l'huom sag- gio ò
Risposta
fug - ge? *fug - ge?* Che co-sa è l'huom che l'cer- ca e cer- ca in-va - no?
Risposta
65
Risposta
*va - no.* Chi da la mor - te al cor con di-spia - ce - re? *pia- ce - re.*

Risposta
Co - me la vi - ta ot - tien, chi vi - ta bra - ma? a - ma.
Risposta
A - ma del mon - do le bel - lez - ze, o Di - o? Di - o. Dun -
- que mor - ra chi'l pia - cer bra - ma, è
Risposta
ve - ro? ve - ro. Hor quel che-il Ciel t'ha det - to,

85
Ec - co io rac-col - go in - tie - ro: Fug - gi va -
90
no pia - cer, a - — ma Dio ve - ro.
11
♯ 17

# 38. Johann Hermann Schein
## Chorale Concerto, *Erschienen ist der herrliche Tag*

As Reformation music developed in the Baroque era, chorale melodies were used as a melodic source of cantus firmi in the same way that the Gregorian repertory was used as a source for composers of Roman Catholic music. With the notable exception of Heinrich Schütz, the German Protestant composers of the early seventeenth century wrote numerous settings of chorale melodies in the new *concertato* style, which combined voices and instruments. The chorale melody served as a cantus firmus which often was treated very freely, as in Example 38, where the original melody (quoted at the end of this commentary) forms the entire material of the composition used in the voices, and even pervades the instrumental bass. It is separated into its various phrases and motives, modified melodically and rhythmically, and developed in a number of different ways. In settings like this one, the composer strove to interpret the meaning of the text associated with the chorale by the way he handled his material; and Schein here certainly conveyed the triumphant mood of the Easter hymn, *Erschienen ist*. The composition is from the second of two books which Schein called collectively his *Opella Nova* (Latin, *opella,* diminutive of *opus*); the books were printed in 1618 and 1627 respectively, and contain a variety of chorale settings.

Schein's setting of *Erschienen ist* has comparatively modest dimensions. It is written for a small group—four performers in all—consisting of two singers (a choice of two sopranos or two tenors is indicated), a bass instrument (again a choice—bassoon or trombone—presumably dependent upon whether men's or women's voices are used in the duet), and the continuo for a keyboard instrument, which might be either an organ or a harpsichord. The medium is thus a sort of vocal counterpart to the instrumental trio sonata. (See *M of M*, No. 39.)

Schein treats each half of the four-phrase chorale as a melodic unit; the first half runs to bar 40, the second half from bar 40 to 78. The final section, where a change of meter takes place, is like a coda, and is based on the Alleluia extension of the last phrase of the chorale.

The two phrases of the beginning, with melodic ornamentation, are delivered in canonic style, the upper voice leading each time; the second time it is followed in close imitation. At bar 22 there is a brief sequential development of the uncolored opening motive of the chorale, followed by a free statement of the phrase-pair leading to a dominant cadence that marks the end of the first section (bar 40). In the next section, phrase three is stated by the upper voice alone, then by the lower voice alone a fifth higher, then by both voices in close imitation. Phrase four follows, also in close imitation. At bar 63 the lower voice takes the lead for the first time, and delivers phrases three and four consecutively, with close imitation by the upper voice. In the final Alleluia section, beginning at the second half of bar 78, the descending four-note scale motive is a rhythmically modified version of the motive to which the word "Alleluia" is set in the chorale tune. Upper and lower voices alternate in taking the lead, then begin together where eighth-notes first enter into the rhythm.

The motives of the melody are often drawn upon for the bass line, where they are sometimes used to set up a point of imitation between the bass and one voice part (as at the very beginning), or among the bass and both voice parts (*e.g.*, bars 29–33). At other times the function of the bass is harmonic only. Schein's figured bass disregards the octave register. The continuo has been realized somewhat more elaborately in this example than in Example 37, and the realization sometimes makes contrapuntal use of motives from the voice parts, in keeping with the general character and texture of the piece.[1]

The hymn and melody of *Erschienen ist* are by Nicolaus Herman, and were first published in his *Die Sontags Evangelia uber das gantze Jar*, Wittenberg, 1560. The melody and text of the first stanza:

[1] Compare Walter's setting of *Komm, Gott Schöpfer*, Example 24 of this book, in which the melody is treated as a long-note cantus firmus. Example 41, by Buxtehude, shows still another manner of handling a chorale melody.

The day hath dawned—the day of days
Transcending all our joy and praise;
This day our Lord triumphant rose;
This day He captive led our foes.
Hallelujah!

(Translation by Arthur T. Russell, *Psalms and Hymns*, No. 113, Cambridge, 1851.)

Source: *Opella Nova, ander Theil Geistlicher Concerten mit 3, 4, 5, und 6 Stimmen zusampt dem General-Bass* . . . Leipzig, 1626.

Modern edition: B. Engelke, *Johann Hermann Schein, Sämtliche Werke*, Vol. VI, p. 115, Leipzig, 1919.

## 38. Johann Hermann Schein (1586–1630)

## Chorale Concerto, *Erschienen ist der herrliche Tag*

Soprano or Tenor
Er- schie- nen ist der herr - li- che Tag, dran sich nie -
Soprano or Tenor
Bassoon or Trombone
mand gnug freu- en mag, der herr - li- che
Er - schie- nen ist der - herr - li- che Tag, dran sich nie -
Tag, er- schie-nen ist der herr - li - che
mand gnug freu - en mag, er-schie-nen ist der

Tag, dran_ sich ___ nie - mand gnug freu - en mag, gnug
herr - li - che Tag, dran_ sich ___ nie - mand gnug freu - - -
freu- en mag. Er- schie-nen ist, er - schie-nen ist,
- - en mag. Er - schie-nen ist, er - schie-nen
er - schie - nen ist der herr - li - che Tag, der herr - li - che,
ist, er - schie-nen ist der herr - li - che Tag, der

herr - li - che Tag, dran sich nie - mand gnug freu - en
herr - li - che Tag, der herr - li- che Tag,
mag, dran sich nie - mand gnug freu - en mag. Christ
dran sich nie - mand gnug freu - en mag.
un - ser Herr heut tri - um - phiert,
Christ un - ser

50
Christ un - ser _ Herr heut
Herr heut ___ tri - um - phiert, Christ un - ser _
6 6 ♯
55
tri - um - phiert, all sein ___ Feind er ge -
Herr heut tri - um - phiert, all sein ___ Feind
60
fan - gen ___ führt, al - le - lu - - - ja,
er ge - fan - gen ___ führt, al - le - lu - ja, al -
4 3 ♯

65
al - le - lu - ja, Christ un - ser
le - lu - - - ja, Christ un - ser Herr heut
4 3(♯) ♯
Herr heut tri - um - phiert, all
tri - um - phiert, all sein Feind
♯ 6 ♯
70
sein Feind er ge - fan - gen führt, al -
er ge - fan - gen führt, al - le - lu - -

le - lu - ja, al - le - lu - - - -

- ja, al - le - lu -

ja, al - le - lu - ja, al - le - lu - - ja,

ja, al - le - lu - ja, al - le - lu - ja, al - le -

al - le - lu - ja, al - le - lu - ja, al - le - lu - ja, al - le -

lu - ja, al - le - lu - - ja, al - le - lu - ja,

85
lu - ja, al - le - lu - ja, al - le - lu - - ja.
al - le - lu - - - - ja.
5 6 ♯ 6 7 3(♯) 6 4 5 3(♯) ♯

# 39. Denis Gaultier

## Lute Piece, *Tombeau de Mademoiselle Gaultier*

The lute arrangement of the frottola, *O mia cieca e dura sorte* (Example 21 of this book), and Example 39, *Tombeau de Mademoiselle Gaultier*, are works for the lute from the beginning and the end of the period during which the lute occupied an important place in Western music. Gaultier was the most distinguished of the French lutenists of the seventeenth century; the *Tombeau* (French, "tomb") is from his celebrated collection of fifty-six compositions which he called the *Rhétorique des Dieux* (the "eloquent language of the gods"), extant in a richly illustrated manuscript made for one of his admirers in 1652.

The arrangement of Example 39 on the page differs from that of any other piece in this present book; a reproduction—in a modern hand—of the tablature in which it appears in the original manuscript has been set above the corresponding notes in the transcription, to illustrate the tablature system in which French lute music was notated, and to make clear the fundamental musical problem involved in transcribing lute music.

The *Rhétorique des Dieux* was arranged by the composer in a succession of suites, each of which comprises a series of movements in the same key. Gaultier called the keys "modes," and used the Greek terms Dorian, Hypodorian, Phrygian, and so on; but there is nothing of a modal character in the music except the general correspondence of "minor" modes to keys of minor tonality. Gaultier followed a new nomenclature adopted in France in the seventeenth century whereby the system of modes began on C, not D. Thus the new Phrygian, untransposed, would be on D, not E; but Gaultier has put the Phrygian pieces in the key of F♯ minor in his tablature. Example 39 is the first piece in the "Phrygian" suite of the *Rhétorique.*

Nearly all the pieces in the collection are dances of a highly stylized character—allemandes, courantes, and sarabandes—set in the most refined style of the traditional lute idiom, in which voices enter and leave freely, single melodic lines alternate with chords, polyphonic texture is suggested, and arpeggiated chords and ornaments abound. (Curiously, the manuscript of the *Rhétorique des Dieux* is almost completely lacking in ornamental signs, although embellishments were expected to be added by the lutenist; those seen in the transcription are ornaments indicated in the five other tablature manuscripts in which the *Tombeau* is also found.)

The *Tombeau,* a composition written in memory of a dead person, is a genre with a long and honored history in French music. It has no specific musical form. Gaultier's piece is actually an idealized allemande, and has the characteristic binary dance form of two evenly balanced sections, marked in the middle by a strong cadence and double bar, with repeats indicated at the end of each section.

There is a certain quality of preciosity and affectation in the *Rhétorique* which is well illustrated in the program note inscribed at the end of the *Tombeau;* this reads, in translation:

> The illustrious Gaultier, favored by the gods with the supreme power of animating bodies without souls, sings on his lute of the sad and lamentable separation of the half of himself, describing it in the Tombeau which he has raised in the noblest part of the other half which remains to him, and has it tell how, like the phoenix, he was given life again in immortalizing this mortal half.

The tablature above the staves in modern notation represents graphically the six strings of the lute, which in Gaultier's time were tuned as shown in Fig. 2; in fact, Gaultier is said to have introduced this tuning.

Fig. 2

The letters on the lines represent the positions (frets) on the strings that were to be stopped by the left hand to obtain the desired pitch, *a* representing the open, unstopped string. Each successive letter after *a* indicates a pitch of a half-step higher; thus on the bottom string *b* = B♭, *c* = B♮, *d* = C, and so on. In addition to these six strings, there were other, lower strings which did not go over the fingerboard and were therefore unchangeable in pitch; these were called the *bass-courses.* The beginning of each of Gaultier's suites indicates how these lower strings were to be tuned (the *accord*), which was done according to the key of the piece. For this piece the tuning of the bass-courses is: $\bar{a}$ = F♯, $\bar{\bar{a}}$ = E, $\bar{\bar{\bar{a}}}$ = D, $\bar{\bar{\bar{\bar{a}}}}$ = C♯. (At bar 15 the player was apparently expected to stop the 2nd bass-course by a half-step to sound the lone E♯ in the bass.) The rhythm is represented by the stems above the brace, each value indicated being continued until a new value appears, beginning with the first note of each measure.

The problem that faces the transcriber of lute tablature has already been referred to in the commentaries to Examples 21 and 34; it concerns the question of whether the note values indicated in the tablature are to be transcribed literally, or whether the polyphonic voice-leading latent in the tablature notation should be written out as such. The *Tombeau* is transcribed in the latter of these two methods; had it been done in the literal manner the beginning would appear as follows:

Source: Berlin, Deutsche Staatsbibliothek, Kupferstichkabinet, Ms. 78. C. 12.
Modern edition: A. Tessier and J. Cordey, *La Rhétorique des Dieux et autre pièces de luth de Denis Gaultier*, Paris, 1932–33, Vols. VI and VII of the Publications de la Société Française de Musicologie. Facsimile of the *Tombeau de Mademoiselle Gaultier* in Vol. VI, p. 27; transcription in Vol. VII, p. 16. Oskar Fleischer, *Vierteljahrschrift für Musikwissenschaft,* 1883, p. 3. Literal transcription of this example on p. 126.

## 39. Denis Gaultier (*ca.* 1603–1672)

### Lute Piece, *Tombeau de Mademoiselle Gaultier*

15
20

# 40. Alessandro Poglietti
# Harpsichord Piece, *Capriccio über dass Hennengeschrey*

In the rapid growth of instrumental music that occurred in the seventeenth century, keyboard music flourished vigorously in every important European center. Of the various forms cultivated—stylized dances, free rhapsodic forms, and forms with continuous imitation—the fugal forms in many ways were the most important for the evolution of keyboard music in the late Baroque, for they were the immediate precursors of the fugue. These fugal forms were the canzona, the ricercar, the fantasia, and the capriccio; their origins lay in keyboard transcriptions of vocal models, the vocal chanson giving rise to the instrumental canzona, and the motet to the ricercar and fantasia. The capriccio was a special type of canzona whose main feature was an unusual subject, often of a descriptive nature, as illustrated in Example 40. These fugal forms, like their vocal forebears, often included a succession of different subjects, each of which was treated in a fugal exposition (see the Canzona, *M of M*, No. 26). Some, however, employed only a single subject which was varied in some manner at the beginning of each exposition (see the ricercar of Frescobaldi, *M of M*, No. 34). A third type, of which Example 40 is an instance, used a single subject which remained unchanged throughout; these compositions are very close to the fugue of the Bach period.

Poglietti was one of a group of keyboard composers active around Vienna in the late seventeenth century; others in this group were Richter, Froberger, Kerl, and Pachelbel. Poglietti, a musician at the court in Vienna, favored pieces of a programmatic character: he wrote a suite depicting the rebellion in Hungary (with appropriate subtitles); a set of variations in which he parodied different national dances, instruments, and customs; and several compositions based on the song of the nightingale. The *Capriccio über dass Hennengeschrey* (*Capriccio on the Cackle of the Hen*) is from a set of three pieces in fugal style, each of which has an amusing and realistic musical imitation of a hen-call as its subject, not dissimilar in character to the main subject of Rameau's *La poule.* The subject of this *Capriccio* may be unique in the entire literature of fugal compositions in having a double note as an essential feature; whenever the subject is delivered integrally the double note is present, with the sole exception of the final statement (bar 46).

The *Capriccio* is susceptible of being analyzed as a fugue from the standpoint of both structure and texture. It has an exposition (bars 1–13) which differs from the more developed type of fugue only in the manner of entry of its four voices—on the tonic, dominant, tonic, and subdominant scale degrees, respectively, instead of the conventional alternation of tonic and dominant entries of the later fugue. In the middle section (bars 14–35), Poglietti uses a series of five subject entries; two of these overlap in the manner of a short stretto (Italian, "close") (bars 14–16, and 29–31); two are single entries (bars 18–19, and 33–34); and one is an entry followed immediately by another in the same voice (bars 22–25). Between these entries are interstitial passages of from one to three bars. In the middle section Poglietti makes a modulation to the dominant at bar 29—by way of the subdominant at bar 25—and remains in it until the concluding section begins at bar 36. (The notation of the original, which is without key signature even though it is in G major, has been retained in the example.) The lack of further modulations, due in part to the restrictions of the system of tuning then in use, is another of the differences between this piece and a fugue of the Bach period. In the concluding section of the *Capriccio* (from bar 36 to the end) the stretto entries occur continuously—bar 40 being the only one in which an entry does not appear—until the last entry of all in bar 45, a procedure that provides a fine climactic drive to the end of the composition.

Source: A manuscript from the beginning of the eighteenth century in the possession of F. Bischoff, Graz, Austria.

Modern editions: H. Botsiber, *Wiener Klavier- und Orgelwerke der zweiten Hälfte des 17. Jahrhunderts, DTÖ*, XIII, ii, p. 37, Vienna, 1906. G. Tagliapietra, *Antologia di musica . . . per pianoforte*, Vol. 8, p. 27, Milan, 1931–32.

## 40. Alessandro Poglietti (d. 1683)

### Harpsichord Piece, *Capriccio über dass Hennengeschrey*

20
25
30
35

40
45

# 41. Dietrich Buxtehude
# Organ Chorale Prelude, *Nun Komm, der Heiden Heiland*

The first German composer to make extensive use of chorale melodies in compositions for organ was Samuel Scheidt. In his *Tabulatura Nova* (1624), he used these tunes as cantus firmi for extended sets of variations, and also treated them as chorale fantasies in which each successive phrase of a chorale melody served as a subject for a fugal exposition. It was not until the generation of Buxtehude that composers set these melodies in chorale preludes—short intimate pieces in which the melody is presented only once, and in such a manner that the mood of the text with which the melody is associated is reinforced by its harmonic and contrapuntal setting. Most of the forty-odd compositions that Buxtehude based on chorales have this character, although he also wrote works on the grander scale of chorale variation and chorale fantasy. The majority of his chorale preludes treat the chorale melody in a manner similar in principle to that of Example 41, *Nun komm, der Heiden Heiland*, in which the melody itself is embellished by the addition of expressive figuration. The tradition of embellishment by German organ composers—formerly called "coloration"—is one that goes back to the fifteenth century (for example, Conrad Paumann's *Fundamentum organisandi*), but most of the colored arrangements of earlier composers make use of an abstract kind of figuration. Buxtehude, however, makes embellishment a prime factor in his subjective musical interpretation of the mood of the chorale.

*Nun komm* is an Advent or Christmas hymn derived directly from the hymn attributed to St. Ambrose, *Veni redemptor gentium* ("Come,

O Saviour of the heathen"), in a translation by Luther himself. The melody traditionally attached to this hymn was somewhat modified by Johann Walter, and the chorale in its present form appeared in the *Geystliche Gesangk Buchleyn* of 1524 (see commentary to Example 24 of this book). The original Latin hymn and melody are given at the end of this commentary; below it, for purposes of comparison, is the Lutheran version on which Buxtehude's chorale prelude is based.

Buxtehude keeps the chorale melody in the upper voice, and states each of its four phrases in progressively richer embellishment on each successive phrase. Generally speaking, each note of the chorale melody that represents a beat occupies a half-bar of the prelude; but at times the chorale notes do not fall so regularly, and at one point are even absent from the upper voice (bar 13; note that the missing tones are in the tenor). The figuration added to the chorale melody is predominantly conjunct, varied by turn and trill figures and a few repeated notes. The line of the melody is made rhythmically sensitive and plastic through the use of a variety of note values and by occasional dotted notes. The last phrase is continued into an elaborately embellished cadence; the previous phrases all come to an end on the last note of the chorale phrase, and are separated from each other by brief passages in which the smooth and majestic flow of counterpoint in the lower voices continues. The three lower voices are in nonimitative counterpoint, and put the chorale variation in high relief by their considerably lesser degree of rhythmic activity. The combined counterpoint of all the voices represents an interesting combination of Aeolian mode and harmonic minor tonality. The opening motive of the chorale is suggested at the sections between phrases and at the second half of bar 4 in the two inner voices.

Buxtehude's setting of this melody differs from J. S. Bach's *Orgelbüchlein* setting in which the melody is stated in relatively unadorned form in the upper voice, against a faster, restlessly moving, freely imitative background in the lower voices (a texture similar to the one employed in the chorale prelude in *M of M*, No. 47). Buxtehude's personal interpretation of the chorale is in keeping with the spirit of the text, which expresses awe and wonder aroused by the contemplation of the miraculous entry of the Lord into the sinful world.

Ve - ni re - demp - tor gen - ti - um, os - ten - de par - tum vir - gi - nis.

Nun komm, der Hei - den Hei - land, Der Jung - frau - en Kind er - kannt,

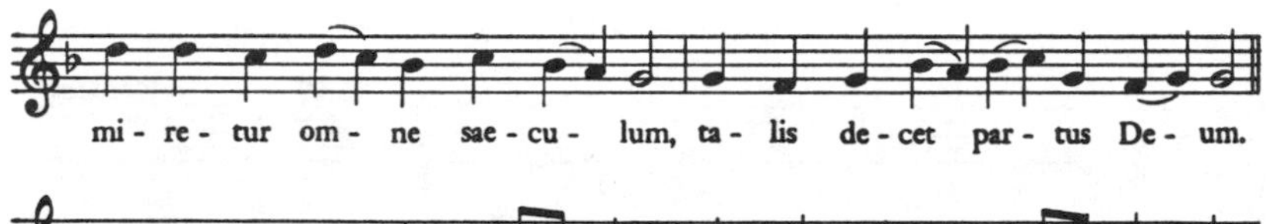
mi - re - tur om - ne sae - cu - lum, ta - lis de - cet par - tus De - um.

Dass sich wun - dert al - le Welt: Gott solch Ge - burt ihm be - stellt.

A translation of the first of the eight verses of the text:

Saviour of the heathen, come,  
Virgin's Son, here make Thy home;  
Wonder at it, heav'n and earth,  
That the Lord chose such a birth.

Source: Berlin, Deutsche Staatsbibliothek, Ms. 22.541.  
Modern edition: P. Spitta, *Dietrich Buxtehudes Werke für Orgel*, Vol. II, p. 124. New edition by M. Seiffert, Leipzig, 1904.

## 41. Dietrich Buxtehude (1637–1707)

## Organ Chorale Prelude: *Nun Komm, der Heiden Heiland*

15
20

# 42. Marc-Antoine Charpentier
## Oratorio Scene from *Le Reniement de St-Pierre*

The first oratorios in the manner in which the form is presently defined —a dramatic work dealing with a religious subject, with recitatives, arias, ensembles, and choruses, but without scenery, costumes, or action —were those of Carissimi. This composer had few followers in Italy, but in France his pupil Charpentier continued to write oratorios in a style similar to his master's, although on a generally larger scale, and with more dramatic effectiveness and greater musical resource. Charpentier introduced the oratorio to France, but he had no successors in the genre there, and his music was quickly forgotten after his death. He has been rediscovered in recent decades, and critical opinion places his oratorios halfway between those of Carissimi and Handel, stylistically as well as chronologically.[1]

Of Charpentier's thirty-four Latin works in this form, fourteen are more elaborate than the others, and are called *Historiae* by their composer. Among these, three are on subjects also treated by Carissimi: *Extremum Dei Judicium* ("The Last Judgment"), *Sacrificium Abrahae* ("Abraham's Sacrifice"), and *Judicium Salomonis* ("The Judgment of Solomon"); Carissimi's setting of the central scene of this last appears in *M of M*, No. 32. Charpentier uses biblical stories for his libretti, treating them in dialogue which is a slightly paraphrased version of the original text.

Example 42 is taken from his best-known oratorio, *Le Reniement de St-Pierre* ("The Denial of Peter"). The action of the whole oratorio begins with the Institution of the Last Supper, and ends at the point where "Peter went out and wept bitterly" (Luke 22:60) after the prophecy about the crowing of the cock has been fulfilled. The events

[1] See H. W. Hitchcock: "The Latin Oratorios of Marc-Antoine Charpentier," *MQ*, 1955, p. 41.

related in this scene are from Matthew 26:69–75 and John 18:25–27.

Example 42 opens with the traditional *historicus*, or narrator. The role is not confined to a single person, but in this scene is taken first by a mixed five-part chorus in homophonic style at the beginning, a bass soloist in recitative style in the middle (bars 25–29), and a duet of women's voices in a brief arioso-like passage at the end (bars 45–48). Charpentier's characterizing style of recitative is clearly illustrated in the passage from bars 21 to 29, within which the declamation of the three persons involved—the suspicious question of the maid, the anguished denial of Peter, and the sober recital of events by the objective historicus—could hardly be more apt. This scene includes the dramatic highpoint of the oratorio, the ensemble that begins at bar 30, in which Peter is tortured by the relentless questioning of the maids and the kinsman of Malchus (Malchus is named in John 18:10 as the high priest's servant whose ear Peter cuts off during the incident of Christ's apprehension). The denial of Peter is made to stand out above the hammering questions of the others, and continues after they have left off, the whole ensemble creating a tense and vivid picture of the bitter, tragically charged scene.

The translation:

*Historicus:* And Peter was brought into the palace, and he sat at the fire with the servants and officers that he might warm himself; and another maid said unto him:
*Maidservant:* And were you not with Jesus of Nazareth?
*Peter:* O woman, I was not, I knew not the man.
*Historicus:* Then a kinsman of him whose ear he [Peter] had cut off questioned him, saying:
*Doorkeeper* and *Maidservant:* Art thou not a Galilean? Surely thou art, for thy speech betrayeth thee . . . Did I not see thee in the garden with him? Surely thou wert . . . Thou art one of the disciples of that man! . . . *Malchus' Kinsman:* Did'st thou not strike Malchus? . . . *Peter:* No, No! I am not! . . . Truly I was not! . . . I know not what ye are saying! . . . I did not know the man! . . .[2]
*Historicus:* And immediately the cock crew.

Source: Paris, Bibliothèque Nationale, $Vm^1$ 1269, pp. 69–89.

Modern edition: *Concerts spirituels* (a series of publications devoted to the history of sacred music in France, edited by A. Guilmant and C. Bordes, with critical and historical notes by A. Pirro and M. Brenet) . . . *publiés* . . . *par la Schola Cantorum* . . . *Troisième livraison,* Paris, n.d.

[2] The several repetitions of the questions and charges hurled at Peter by the two maids and Malchus' kinsman that occur in the ensemble, and Peter's repeated denials, are not included in the translation.

## 42. Marc Antoine Charpentier (1634–1704)

## Oratorio Scene from *Le Reniement de St-Pierre*

ser - vis et mi - ni - stris ut ca - le - fa - ce- ret se,
ut ca - le - fa - ce- ret se,
ser - vis et mi- ni - stris a - li- a
ut ca - le - fa - ce- ret se,
ser - vis et mi- ni - stris
a - li - a ser - va sic a - it il - li:
a - li - a ser - va sic a - it il - li:
ser - va, a - li - a ser - va sic a - it il - li:
a - li - a ser - va sic a - it il - li:
a - li - a ser - va sic a - it il - li:

Ancilla
Petrus
Et tu cum Je - su Na - za - re - no e - ras? O
♭ 7 6
mu - li - er non e - ram, non no - vi, non no - vi ho - mi-
25
Historicus
nem. Tunc in - ter - ro - ga - vit e - um co - gna - tus
. e - jus cu - jus ab - sci - dit au - ri - cu - lam, di - - cens:

Ostiaria
30
Non - ne tu Ga - li - lae - us es?
Ancilla
Non - ne tu Ga - li -
Petrus
Non, non,
Non - ne te vi - di in hor - to cum e - o? Non-ne tu
Cognatus Malchi
Ve- re tu es,
lae - us es? Ve- re tu es
non sum, non sum, Ve - re non
per - cus - sis - ti Mal - chum? Ve- re tu e - ras
♮6

tu e- ras, Non-ne tu
tu e- ras,
e- ram, ne-sci-o quid di- ci-tis,
tu e- ras, Non-ne tu
Ga-li- lae- us es? Non-ne te vi- di in hor-to cum
35
Non-ne te vi- di in hor-to cum
non sum, non sum, Non, non
Ga-li- lae- us es?
♮4

e - o? Non-ne tu Ga - li - lae - us es? Ve - re tu
e - o? Non-ne tu Ga - li - lae - us es? Ve - re tu
sum. Non sum, non e - ram,
Non - ne te vi - di in hor - to cum e - o?
es, ve - re tu e - ras,
es, Ve - re tu e - ras,
non sum, Ve - re non e - ram, ne - sci -
Ve - re tu e - ras, tu e - ras,

nam et lo - que - la tu - a ma - ni - fes - tum te
40
nam et lo - que - la tu - a ma - ni - fes - tum te
o quid di - ci - tis, non sum, non e - ram, ne-sci-
nam et lo - que - la tu - a ma - ni - fes - tum te
5
6
fa - cit, tu ex di - sci - pu - lus ho - mi - nis is - ti - us
fa - cit, tu ex di - sci - pu - lus ho - mi - nis is - ti - us
o quid di - ci - tis.
Non
fa - cit, tu ex di - sci - pu - lus ho - mi - nis is - ti - us

es.
es.
sum, non fu - i, non e - ram, ne- sci - o quid di - ci- tis, non
es.
45
Historicus
Et con - ti - nu- o gal -
no- vi ho - mi- nem.

Et con - ti - nu - o gal - - - lus can-ta - vit.
- lus can-ta - vit, gal - - lus can-ta - vit.

# 43. John Blow
## Anglican Canticle, *Jubilate Deo*

In the Anglican liturgy for Morning Prayer there are five *canticles*—hymns, generally from the Scriptures and used in church services—that may be set to music: *Venite, Te Deum* and its alternative *Benedicite, Benedictus* and its alternative *Jubilate Deo.* (The Latin incipits for these canticles have remained in use, even though the texts are said or sung in English.) The setting of the canticles for Morning and Evening Prayer and Holy Communion is called the Service, or Full Service when it includes all three canticles; the various canticles of any given Service or Full Service are written in the same key. The history of service music goes back to Tye and Tallis (see commentary to Example 27), both of whom set the canticles in syllabic, homophonic style, following Archbishop Cranmer's advice that in musical settings of the ritual there should be, as far as possible, "for every syllable a note" (see Cranmer's letter to Henry VIII, *SR*, p. 350). This kind of setting was called the "short" service. Later composers such as Byrd, Morley, Weelkes, and Tomkins wrote more elaborate settings in which they used repetition of words and phrases of the text, and a more melismatic, contrapuntal musical texture; this kind of setting was called the "great" service. Composers of the Restoration period, like Blow and Purcell, preferred the syllabic style of the short service; their musical style varies from the purely homophonic through the freely imitative to the strictly canonic.

Blow wrote a great deal of music for the Anglican liturgy, including more than a dozen services. His *Service in G*, from which Example 43 is taken, includes two items each for Morning and Evening Prayer and Communion. The text of *Jubilate* is the 100th Psalm, which is said or sung between the Second Lesson and the Creed in Morning Prayer. This canticle was favored by Restoration composers over *Benedictus*, a reversal of the preference of Elizabethan composers. Blow included the *Gloria Patri* in his setting; this portion of the music and text (bar 43 to end) is engraved on his monument in Westminster Abbey.

In the *Jubilate*, Blow achieves different colors by varying the musical texture and by employing different forces in each of the sections of the work. The opening section (bars 1–20) is sung by two choirs. The choir on the north side of the chancel is called the *cantoris* choir—on the side of the cantor or precentor. The choir on the south, or "deacon's side" is called the *decani* choir. The second section (bars 21–31) is sung by a quartet of solo voices of the cantoris choir, as indicated by the rubric "Verse Cantoris"; the third section (bars 31–42) is sung by the whole choir on the decani side ("Chorus Decani"); while the *Gloria Patri* (bar 43) is sung by both choirs ("Full"). The alternation of choirs is a feature present from the earliest services.

The first section of Example 43 begins chordally, and is followed by three points of imitation at the three successive phrases of the text (bars 4, 8, and 16), in the manner of a motet; the last two begin with simultaneous entries in two voices. The section with the rubric "Canon four in two" (bar 21) is a double canon, one subject being taken by Soprano and Tenor, the other by Alto and Bass. The third section (bar 31) returns to the homophonic texture of the beginning, but a point of imitation is taken up at the phrase "and his truth endureth" (bar 35) and continued to the end of the section. The *Gloria Patri* is a strict canon for all four voices (note the rubric "Canon four in one").

Blow's free-ranging melody, with its characteristically English predilection for frequent skips, creates a fine animation. Cross-relations abound, some the result of an occasional rough-shod drive of counterpoint. In the original score there is a figured organ continuo on a separate staff below the bass which is identical with the bass except for an occasional simplification; when the bass is silent this continuo is the lowest part. The continuo is not an essential part of the musical texture and has not been included in the score. The following remark occurs in an early (1788) printed edition of Blow's *Service in G:* "The Chorus Parts of the following pieces are generally performed in a moderately brisk Time; but where the Verses are introduced, they are play'd considerably slower."

Sources: British Museum, Add. Ms. 17.839 and Harl. Ms. 7338. Boyce's *Cathedral Music*, Vol. I, p. 261, London, 1788. The title of this Service is "The *Te Deum*, *Jubilate*, *Kyrie Eleison*, *Nicene Creed*, *Magnificat*, and *Nunc Dimittis*, as composed in the Key of G with the Greater Third."

## 43. John Blow (*ca.* 1648–1708)

### Anglican Canticle, *Jubilate Deo*

God; it is he that hath made us, and not
it is he that hath made us, and
hath made us, it is he that hath
made us, it is he that hath made us, and
we our-selves; we are his peo - ple,
not we our - - selves; we are his
made us, and not we our-selves; we are his peo - ple,
not we our - selves; we are his
and the sheep, and the sheep of his pas-ture, of his pas - ture.
peo - ple, and the sheep, the sheep of his pas - ture.
and the sheep of his pas - ture, his pas - ture.
peo - ple, and the sheep of his pas - ture.
O go your way in-to his gates with thanks-giv - ing,
O go your way in - to his gates with thanks-
Verse Cantoris
Canon four in two
O go your way in - to his
O go your way in - to his
and in - to his courts with praise; be
giv - ing, and in - to his courts with
gates with thanks-giv - ing, and in - to his
gates with thanks-giv - ing, and

thank - ful un - to him, and speak good
praise; be thank - ful un - to him,
courts with praise; be thank - ful un - to
in - to his courts with praise; be thank - ful
of his Name, and speak good of his Name, of his
and speak good of his Name, and speak good of his
him, and speak good of his Name, and speak good of his
un - to him, and speak good of his Name, of his
Name. Chorus Decani For the Lord is gra - cious, his
Name. For the Lord is gra - cious, his
Name. For the Lord is gra - cious, his
Name. For the Lord is gra - cious, his
mer - cy is e - ver - last - ing; and his
mer - cy is e - ver - last - ing;
mer - cy is e - ver - last - ing;
mer - cy is e - ver - last - ing;
truth en - du - reth, his truth en - du - reth from
and his truth en - du - reth, from
and his truth en - du - reth, from ge - ne - ra -
and his truth en - du - reth, from ge - ne -

ge - ne - ra - - tion, his truth en - du -
ge - ne - ra - - tion, his
tion, his truth en- du - reth from
ra - - - - - tion, his truth en -
40
reth from ge - ne - ra - tion to ge - ne -
truth en- du - reth from ge - ne - ra - tion to
ge - ne - ra - tion
du - reth from ge - ne - ra - tion
ra - - tion. Glo - ry be to the Fa - ther, and
Full
ge - ne - ra - - tion. Glo - ry
to ge - ne - ra - tion. Canon four in one Glo - -
to ge - ne - ra - tion.
45
to the Son, and to the
be to the Fa - ther, and to the Son,
- ry be to the Fa - ther, and to the
Glo - - ry be to the
Ho - ly Ghost, the Ho - ly Ghost; as it
and to the Ho - ly Ghost, the
Son, and to the Ho - ly
Fa - ther, and to the Son, and

was in the be - gin - ning, is now,
50
Ho - ly Ghost; as it was in the be -
Ghost, the Ho - ly Ghost; as it was in
to the Ho - ly Ghost, the Ho - ly
is now, and e - ver shall be, shall
gin - ning, is now, is now, and e -
the be - gin - ning, is now, is now, __
Ghost; as it was in the be - gin - ning,
be, world with - out end. A - - -
- ver shall be, shall be, world with - out
and e - ver shall be, shall be, world
is now, is now, and e - ver shall
55
men, world with - out end. A - - - men.
end. A - - - men, A - - - men.
with - out end. A - - - men, A - - men.
be, shall be, world with - out end. A - - - men.

# 44. Alessandro Scarlatti
# Italian Overture, Sinfonia to *La Caduta de Decem Viri*

This example and the two immediately following represent various aspects of Italian, French, and German opera of the late seventeenth and early eighteenth centuries, two being types of instrumental music used in the opera of that period. Example 44 is a characteristic Italian overture or *sinfonia*, as it was usually called. When it served as an introductory work to a stage piece, as Example 44 did, it was called *Sinfonia avanti l'opera* ("Symphony before the opera").

The history of the opera overture begins with the simple opening fanfare of Monteverdi's *Orfeo*, which he called a toccata. The composers of the Venetian school used the three-sectioned canzona as an overture (for an example by Cesti, see *GMB*, No. 202), and sometimes a canzona of two sections—a slow section followed by one in rapid tempo; this last was the prototype of the Lullian French overture (see *M of M*, No. 36). Alessandro Scarlatti established the Italian style of overture, for which he borrowed the form and style of the concerto grosso, retaining something of the canzona in the smaller framework of the sinfonia. Both the French overture and the Italian sinfonia flourished during the first half of the eighteenth century; the French form became obsolete about the middle of the century, but the sinfonia had the elements of style and structure from which the classical symphony developed. The frankly homophonic Italian form proved to be a pliant and adaptable medium of almost unlimited potentiality in the hands of the classical symphonists.

The opera from which the present example is taken was first performed in Naples in 1697, and was probably composed in that year; if so, it would be a middle-period work in Scarlatti's operatic career. The libretto of the opera, written by Silvio Stampiglia, is based on an actual event in Roman history which took place in 446 B.C., and is described in Livy's *History of Rome*. The overture does not suggest anything of the opening mood of the opera, nor does it make use of any of the melodic material in the work, as later came to be done. Tempo marks are lacking, but it was understood that the three sections of a sinfonia were in the relation of Allegro-Adagio-Allegro (or Presto). The close relationship with the concerto grosso is implied by the presence of the words *solo* and *soli* at the entries of the first and second violins in the first bar; in another manuscript copy of this opera the word *tutti* occurs at the entrance of the whole string orchestra at bar 4. The bass of the first section is lacking in figures except for those in bars 17 and 18.

Each of the three sections of the piece is in a binary form; in the second and third sections a strong cadence and a double-bar sign mark the middle of each section. The first section is far less obviously articulated, however. Its first half, which goes up to the beginning of bar 16, consists of two motives: the brisk rising figure shared by the two solo violins at the beginning, and the repeated-note figure followed by an octave drop that starts in the middle of bar 5. After a quick modulation at bar 7, the same material is heard again in the dominant key, returning to the tonic during the two-bar extension of the second figure. The second half of this section is in three-bar phrasing throughout, beginning with a brilliant passage in thirds by the solo violins during which the dominant is reached. In the next phrase (bars 19–21) the repeated-note figure of the first half of this section is brought back, and the tonality moves to the relative minor. The third phrase (bars 22–24) is a sequential repetition of the second phrase, and returns to the tonic, while the last phrase (bars 25 to end) brings back the passage in thirds of the first phrase. The clear but intricate design of the little piece may be represented thus: *a*, *b*, *a′* *b′*, *c* *b″*, *b‴* *c′*.

The second section, in the key of the dominant, is featured by chains of suspensions, a common trait in the slow movements of the concerto. The last section, returning to B-flat, is a rollicking gigue, with an extension of the second half by an echo effect at the place where the composer has put the word "piano." The last section ends with the same rising motive with which the first section began. The composition is significant for its time in the use of tonality as a form-defining element through key contrast, and also in the related occurrence of periodic structure.

The E-flat in the key signature of the first and third sections is an editorial addition; in the manuscript the signature is one flat throughout all three sections, E-flat being added in the staves wherever necessary.

Source: A manuscript copy of the opera in the Vassar College Music Library, Poughkeepsie, N. Y., undated, but in a hand of the period in which the opera was written.

## 44. Alessando Scarlatti (1659–1725)

## Italian Overture, Sinfonia to *La Caduta de Decem Viri*

15
6
6
20

25
(Adagio)
30
Piano
7 6 4 6 9 4 4 3
35
40
9 5 4 0 6 ♮ 6 4 3 ♮

45
6 4 6 4 ♯ 6 ♯ 6 6 5 6 ♭
50
6 5 6 6 5 4 6 6 5 4 3
(Presto)
55
12 8
6 6 6
9 8 6 5 9 8
60
♭5

65
70
(Piano)

5
4
6
6

# 45. André Campra
# Chaconne from the Opera-Ballet *Les Fêtes Vénitiennes*

In establishing the form and character of the French opera, Lully gave an important role to the ballet; his stage works have many scenes called *entrées* which do little to further the action of the opera, but which do embellish it with elaborate ballet spectacles. After Lully's death a new French stage form came into being—the *opera-ballet;* it consisted of a series of entrées, each of which was expanded through the addition of arias, recitatives, and choruses into the equivalent of an act. Each entré had its own slight story which was not connected with the other entrées in plot or characters; however, there was usually some very general theme running through the whole. The first opera-ballets were those of Pascal Colasse (*Ballet des Saisons*, 1695) and André Campra (*L'Europe galante*, 1697). Campra was the most important French opera writer between Lully and Rameau. In 1710 his opera-ballet *Les Fêtes Vénitiennes*, on a libretto by A. Danchel, was performed with enormous success, and held its place in the repertory of the Paris Opera for over a half-century. One reason for its long life was its flexible form, which allowed for the substitution or addition of new entrées without affecting the piece as a whole.

Following Lully's usual practice, Campra made the final dance of the final (third) entrée of his opera-ballet a chaconne—given here as Example 45. In later productions of this work the number of entrées was extended to five, and this one—called *L'Amour Saltimbanque* ("Love the mountebank")—was made the second entrée. The various entrées are united only by common setting and subject—they all deal in a highly artificial but charming way with the subject of love affairs during Carnival time in Venice.

The chaconne, originally a dance in triple meter in moderately slow time, was a favored form of Baroque composers for both vocal and instrumental music. It consists of a series of continuous variations proceeding in the same motion as the original dance. The variations were not founded on a specific theme but on a sort of generalized bass figure of four bars which descended over the upper four notes of the scale, either directly or in some variant like the one of the first phrase of Campra's chaconne. The essence of the chaconne is the repetition of this bass pattern throughout the composition with continual melodic or rhythmic variations upon the several repetitions of the pattern. The chaconne is related to the passacaglia in its general structure of continuous variations, but the passacaglia is based on an ostinato figure that usually remains unchanged through the composition. It must be added, however, that the two terms were used indiscriminately in the Baroque era, and the distinction made here is one that has come to be used in modern times for convenience in classification. It will also be noted that the chaconne is related in principle to the late Renaissance passamezzo (see Example 35).

Campra's chaconne proceeds throughout in pairs of four-bar phrases in which the chaconne figure and the melody and harmony above it are first repeated and then followed by a variation of the bass figure with a new melody, in turn repeated, and so on. A strong cadence, with hemiola rhythm in the bass, brings the first section to an end at the double bar (measure 33). After three more phrase-pairs the tonality changes to the parallel minor, and the melodic direction of the chaconne bass is reversed. At bars 73 and 81 still further variations of the bass occur, and a return to the original key is made at bar 89. It is at this point that the simplest form of the chaconne bass occurs, followed immediately by a variation with the liveliest figuration in the piece. The words *jusqu'au mot FIN* ("up to the word *ending*") indicate a return to the beginning, so that the piece ends at the double bar of measure 33. Thus the over-all design is *A-B-A'-A*.

Source: *Les Festes vénitiennes, Ballet mis en musique par Monsieur Campra . . . Paris, chez Christophe Ballard* . . . , p. 61, 1714.

Modern edition: A. Pougin and A. Guilmant, *Les Festes Vénitiennes, Opera Ballet en 5 Entrées et I Prologue*, p. 129, Paris, 1881.

## 45. André Campra (1660–1744)

## Chaconne from the Opera-Ballet *Les Fêtes Vénitiennes*

30
6 6
Fin
35
7 7
40
tr
45
7 6♯
tr
50

tr
55
60
4 3 6 4 3♯
65
5 6♭ 6 6♭
4 3
70
4 3♯
6♭
tr
75
6 4 3♯

80
85
tr
tr
90
95

100
Jus qu'au mot Fin
tr
105

# 46. Reinhard Keiser
## Aria, "Hoffe noch," from *Croesus*

Opera in Germany began as Italian opera in the courts of such centers as Munich, Vienna, and Dresden. However, the German free cities encouraged opera in the German language by German composers, particularly in Hamburg, where a public opera house was established in 1678. The leading light of the Hamburg opera was Reinhard Keiser, who is said to have written over a hundred operas during his long period of activity there as composer and manager of the Opera. Of the twenty-five operas by him that are preserved, *Croesus* (from which Example 46 is taken) is generally regarded as his masterpiece. In it there are obvious traces of Italian opera in the treatment of the solo voice, and of French style in the instrumental music of the overture and the occasional entrées; German operatic practice is followed in the insertion of strophic songs of popular character in local dialect. Beyond these features, however, a personal musical style of a high order is manifested in Keiser's imaginative shaping of motives and his mastery in handling them, his freedom in using conventional forms, his resource of instrumental coloring, and his expressive use of rhythm. These traits can be seen in the aria from *Croesus*, "Hoffe noch"; they are the reason why Keiser was held in the highest esteem by the musicians of his period.

The opera *Croesus* is based on an incident from Herodotus's account of the Persian wars in which the Lydian king, Croesus, was captured and condemned to death by Cyrus the Great of Persia. The story was fantastically embellished and given a happy ending by the Italian poet Minato, whose libretto was set by fifteen other opera composers beside Keiser, including Draghi (the first to set it, in 1678), Hasse, Jommelli, and Legrenzi. Keiser's version was a translation, and in part a revision, by Bostel; his opera was first performed at Hamburg in 1710. The aria "Hoffe noch" is sung by Elmira, a Medean princess in love with Atis, Croesus' son. "Hoffe noch" occurs at the beginning of the second scene of Act I, and is a tender portrayal of the troubled and changing moods of love in the heart of a young girl.

"Hoffe noch" is a da capo aria. In the original score the da capo repeat is written out, but in the music of Example 46 a return is made from the end to bar 17, where the first part of the aria is taken up to the word *Fine*, bar 52. The smaller notes in measures 17, 25, 29, 30, 31, 38, 41, and 42 are several slight modifications that Keiser made in the vocal and instrumental parts for the repeat. The mood of the aria is very beautifully set at the opening by a sighing motive descending sequentially through tonalities that change at every two bars. The mood is enhanced by the instrumental coloring and the give-and-take of solo oboe and unison violins from bar 9 to the end of the introduction. The initial theme is stated again at the entry of the voice in a subtly varied interplay between voice and oboe.

Keiser gives variety to the accompaniment throughout by the simplest means—by having oboe or violins play alone for a few bars, or in unison, or in alternation, or by keeping the violins to a background figure while the oboe and voice carry on a duet. Variety is contributed also by the continuo, which sometimes drops out of the ensemble temporarily, and in one case doubles the oboes and violins at the lower octave (bars 78–81, where the voice joins the upper instruments in unison).

The voice is sometimes given passages of a distinctly instrumental idiom, as in bars 26–30 on the word "hoffe," and the whole section of bars 71–81 with its lively treatment of the word "Scherz." The entire *Allegro assai* middle section, with its change to *andante* for seven bars beginning at bar 64, is an especially fine instance of Keiser's word-painting and poetic rendering of the changing moods of Elmira; the melisma on "bange" ("troubled") is particularly expressive. Throughout the aria the affinity of voice and oboe is intimate and sensitive, with continual changes of textural relationship which are in turn freely contrapuntal, unisonic, and in parallel thirds and sixths; the writing even includes an echo (bars 53–56). The whole aria is a happy balance of expressive content and consummate craftsmanship.

Translation of the text:

Hope yet, vexed heart.
Fear and grief cast down my trust.

But love consoles me,
And raises me up again.
Sometimes after my troubled mood
Pleasure and jesting quickly follow.

Source: Berlin, Deutsche Staatsbibliothek. Manuscript copy of the score with title page: *Croesus, Drama Musicale da rappresentarsi nel Teatro Hamburgo, Anno 1710.* The first printed libretto carries the full title of the opera: *Der hochmütige, gestürtzte und wieder erhabene Croesus* . . . Hamburg, 1711.

Modern edition: M. Schneider, *DDT*, Bd. XXXVII–XXXVIII, p. 17, Leipzig, 1912. This edition includes the changes made in the score by Keiser for a revival of the opera in 1730. Among them is the substitution of an Italian sinfonia for the French overture of the original version.

## 46. Reinhard Keiser (1674–1739)

## Aria, "Hoffe noch," from *Croesus*

20
noch, hof - fe noch, ge-kränk-tes
6
6
Herz, hof - fe noch, hof - -
25
1)
tutti
2)
30
fe, hof - fe
forte
tutti
5 ♮
1)
2)

35
noch, ge - kränk - tes Herz, ge - kränk - - - tes Herz!
40
45
Furcht und Schmerz,
Furcht und Schmerz war - fen mein Ver - trau - en nie -
tr
f

50
Fine
Allegro assai
der.
Doch die Lie - be
tr
tr
Allegro assai
6
55
trö - - stet mich,
tr
6
6
6
doch die Lie - be trö - - stet mich trö-stet und er-hebt
6
60
mich wie - der. Manch - mal,
tr

Andante
65
manch- mal folgt auf ban - ge Trie- be, auf ban - - -
piano
70
- - - ge Trie - be
Allegro
plötz- lich wie- der Lust und Scherz,
forte
Allegro
75

plötz - lich wie - der Lust und
80
Dal 𝄋 al Fine
Scherz.

# 47. Antonio Vivaldi
## Solo Concerto, *La Primavera* (1st Movement)

Antonio Vivaldi, a prolific composer of operas, oratorios, and cantatas, is known chiefly for his concertos; he wrote over four hundred, including both the older type of the concerto grosso and the then newer solo concerto in which a solo instrument, most often a violin, replaced the concertino group of soloists, whose usual make-up was two violins and a cello. The establishment of the solo concerto was due largely to Torelli; in the fast movements he restricted the tutti groups to a precise and easily remembered theme which is first stated in full, then is heard in part several times during the course of the movement, alternating with episodes in which the solo violin has passages of brilliant figuration. This description applies to the two outer movements of the concerto; the slow movement between them is organized differently. Like the sinfonia and the concerto grosso, the solo concerto kept to a generally homophonic texture.

Example 47 is the opening movement of the well-known concerto *La Primavera*, the first of a set of twelve solo concertos, Opus 8, published in Antwerp about 1725, to which Vivaldi gave the name *Il Cimento dell'armonia e dell'inventione* ("The Trial of Harmony and Invention"; "Invention" may apply to the special descriptive effects used in several of these works). The first four concertos of the set are called collectively *Le Stagioni* ("The Seasons"). Each season is described in a poem, the lines of which are printed in the music at appropriate places. The first movement, whose explanatory poem is given in translation at the end of this commentary, is followed by a slow movement which depicts a pastoral scene in which the inserted lines describe a goatherd sleeping in a pleasant meadow with his dog at his side. The last movement portrays a dance of nymphs and shepherds to the sound of bagpipes. The concertos of the other seasons are *L'Estate* ("Summer"), *L'Autunno* ("Autumn"), and *L'Inverno* ("Winter").

Vivaldi has poetically exploited the concerto style and its flexible design to fit his programme, not only in its broad outlines from movement to movement, but even more ingeniously within each movement. In Example 47, for instance, the mood of awakening spring is established by the happy, easily remembered opening tutti and reasserted at each return of this theme; the solo episodes are those in which the vernal images are evoked and for which the poetic lines are supplied. There are two exceptions to this general scheme—the opening tutti has a phrase of the added text, and the last solo episode (beginning in the middle of bar 70) has none—but these exceptions are readily accounted for; the first by the composer's desire to state immediately the basic subject of the poetic programme, the other by its special position in the concerto structure, as explained below.

The tutti theme consists of two phrases (bars 1–3, and 7–10), each of which is immediately repeated in the manner of an echo and is then followed by a cadencing motive. There is a pleasing asymmetry to the phrasing, phrase *a* being three bars long, phrase *b* four bars. In the next three appearances of the tutti theme (bars 28–30, 41–43, 56–58) only the *b* phrase is stated, and without the echo repetition. At bar 66 the *a* theme returns, and the section from here to the end should be considered as one complete tutti statement balancing the complete tutti statement of the opening. There is one difference: a final solo episode is interpolated between phrases *a* and *b* (bars 70–75) which was a common practice in the concerto (a similar instance appears in the Handel Concerto Grosso movement, *M of M*, No. 43). The position and function of this solo episode as a part of the final tutti exempt it from being considered another descriptive scene, and also determine its more abstractly musical character.

Between the first and last tutti statements are four solo episodes, each of which is made engagingly descriptive of typical spring scenes by the imaginative use of appropriate idiomatic figures—the song of birds (bars 13–27), the murmuring of streams (bars 31–40), a thunderstorm (bars 44–55), and the return of the birds (bars 59–65). The tonal plan is clear and straightforward and characteristic of Vivaldi's style.

Changes of tonality are brought about only during the solo passages, and reaffirmed in the tutti. During the second episode the dominant is established; the next episode is modulatory, settling in the relative minor, while the fourth brings the tonality back to the original key.

The music of Example 47 has been arranged on two staves from a score which includes a *violino principale*, a ripieno ("full") string orchestra of first and second violins, violas, cellos, and contrabasses, and the continuo. In the tutti passages the soloist plays the same music as the first violinists of the *ripieno* group; in the solo episodes it may be distinguished as the highest part in the upper staff.

The translation of the poem printed in the score:

*Bar 1:* Spring has come
*Bar 21:* and the birds greet her with merry song
*Bar 31:* and the streams flow with soft murmuring to the breath of zephyrs meanwhile
*Bar 44:* the air being covered with black, lightning and thunder are chosen to proclaim her
*Bar 59:* then, these having quieted, the little birds return to their charming singing.

Source: *Opera VIII, Il Cimento dell'Armonia e dell'Inventione*, Amsterdam (Le Cène, pub.), *ca.* 1725.
Modern edition: G. Malipiero, Edition of Vivaldi's works published by the *Istituto Italiano Antonio Vivaldi,* Tomo 76, Milan, 1950.

# 47. Antonio Vivaldi (*ca.* 1678–1741)
## Solo Concerto, *La Primavera* (1st Movement)

20
e festosetti
la salutan gli Augei con lieto canto
25

tr
tr
tr
tr
(with Cb.)
30
tr
6
4
5
3
6
4
5
3
6
4
5
3
(without Cb.)
Scorrono i fonti
p E i fonti allo spirar de Zeffiretti
Con dolce mormorio
scorrono intanto
35

(with Cb.)
Tuoni
Vengon coprendo l'aer di nero amanto
E lampi, e tuoni ad annuntiarla eletti
(without Cb.)

6
5
50
6
5
5
4
3#

55
(with Cb.)
6 4
5 3
(V. prin.)
tr
(?)
6 4
5 3
6 4
5 3
Canto d'Ucelli
Indi, tacendo
(without Cb.)
60
tr
(V. I, solo)
questi, gli Augelletti tornan di nuovo al lor
Canoro incanto
tr
(V. II, solo)
65
tr
tr
tr
tr

7
7
70
75
tr
(with Cb.)
6
4
5
3

tr
p
6
4
5
3
6
4
5
3
80
tr
6
4
5
3
6
4
5
3
6
4
5
3

# 48. Georg Philipp Telemann
## *Fantasie* for Violin Solo

A small but important category of Baroque instrumental music is the repertory of compositions written for a solo violin, without accompaniment. The existing literature in this category begins with a *Passacaglia* written before 1681 by Biber, and is crowned by Bach's *Six Sonatas and Suites*, written in Cöthen about 1720. German works for violin alone are characterized by polyphonic writing, which was made possible by the fact that the violin then had a lower bridge and bow of lesser tension than the violin of today. Telemann, who was municipal director of music at Hamburg for more than half his long life, contributed a set of twelve *Fantasies* to the solo repertory, which were composed in or before 1735. Example 48 is the fourth Fantasie of this set. Telemann wrote pieces of similar character for solo flute and for harpsichord, which he also called Fantasies.

The solo violin fantasies of Telemann are original in style and ideas, although they are obviously closely related to the Italian sonata and concerto in outline and structure. Most of them follow the three movement fast-slow-fast plan of Example 48, although some have four movements: slow-fast-slow-fast. Many of the slow movements, like the one of this fantasy, are little more than short transitions in a near-related key between the outer fast movements; and most of the last movements, like this one, are dances. A particular feature of German violin music is prominent in this fantasie—its predilection for polyphony and chords produced by the use of double-stopping. Although Telemann was not noted as a violinist he thoroughly understood the technique of the instrument, and the double-stopping that is employed almost continuously in this fantasie is very skillfully and idiomatically managed.

The structure of the opening *Vivace* is strikingly akin to the first movement of a concerto grosso or solo concerto of the Baroque period, largely because of the recurrent statement of the opening section, which returns thrice more during the course of the movement (beginning at bars 15, 34, and 57) and so is generally comparable to the tutti theme of a concerto. These sections also establish the principal key areas traversed—tonic, dominant, subdominant, and tonic. Between the statements of the "tutti" are episodes of different material which are livelier in rhythmical character, thus furthering the resemblance to the concerto, in which such passages represent the solo element. The episodes differ from the principal section by the use of virtuoso figures, and also by the fact that these figures are extended by sequence, a device that occurs only once in the principal section (in the third statement of the principal section, where there is a sequential repetition of the first two bars, 34–37). In the second of these episodes (bars 21–33) a striking climax is achieved just before the cadence in the passage of bars 29–32, during which two melodic lines are projected contrapuntally, one ascending stepwise, the other descending and then proceeding by leaps. The third episode (bars 42–56) joins the material of the two previous episodes, and in the same order in which they first occurred. A final episode (bars 63–72) is in the nature of a brilliant coda; it appears to be entirely new material, but is actually a varied version of the first episode (bars 7–14) extended by a final cadence. The movement recalls the *Italian Concerto* by Bach in that it is a transference to a solo instrument of the form and style of the concerto for a solo instrument and a tutti group.

The *Grave* interlude in the relative minor, though brief, is given definite musical character by its solemn dotted-note rhythm, its cadenza, and its full harmony. Four-note chords are employed wherever the melodic range allows; when the upper voice must be taken on the *a* string, the chords are necessarily limited to three notes.

The *Allegro* finale is a straightforward gigue, whose outstanding features are its buoyant rhythm and its very effective use of double-stops. The concerto principle is absent, and its general musical outline is the usual bipartite suite dance. Echo effects are suggested in bars 6–7, 14–15, and 18–19.

Source: Marburg, Westdeutsche Bibliothek, Hds. 21.786.
Modern edition: G. Hausswald, *Georg Philipp Telemann, Musikalische Werke, Bd. VI* (*Kammermusik ohne Generalbass*), p. 34, Kassel, 1955.

48. Georg Philipp Telemann (1681–1767)

*Fantasie* for Violin Solo

40
45
tr
50
55
60
tr
65
70
tr
Grave
tr
tr
tr
tr
tr
3
3
5

tr
Allegro
5
10
tr
15
20

25

# 49. Benedetto Marcello
# Second Recitative and Aria, Cantata da Camera "Amor tu sei," from *Stravaganze d'Amore*

The final two examples in this book are both arias with preceding recitatives by two important Italian composers of the first half of the eighteenth century, which illustrate two important forms. Example 49 is from a *cantata da camera* ("chamber cantata"), Example 50 from an *opera buffa* ("comic opera").

The chamber cantata, like the opera and the oratorio, was a product of the Italian monody of the early seventeenth century (the name first appears in 1720, in Grandi's *Cantade et arie*) and it developed a similar differentiation between aria and recitative. The chamber cantata eventually became a lyrical, pastoral, or dramatic scene unfolded in a series of da capo arias—usually three—each of which was preceded by a recitative. Most chamber cantatas are for a solo voice with harpsichord continuo, although in some the soloist is replaced by a duet or trio of singers. Since chamber cantatas were written for the delight of a select circle of connoisseurs rather than for a large popular audience it is not surprising that many of them have extraordinary traits of harmony, melody, and occasionally of rhythm. Some are frankly experimental, others even bizarre. The cantata of Marcello from which Example 49 is taken has some very unusual features, yet at the same time is a most attractive and characteristic example of the genre.

The example consists of the second of three recitatives and arias that make up the cantata *Stravaganze d'Amore*. The music, like the text, has a number of "extravagances," and a first glance at the example is apt to be disturbing; the composer has not only dispensed with key signatures, but has deliberately written the music so that wherever flats are used in the voice part, sharps are used enharmonically in the (unfigured) continuo. At times the notation is changed so that sharps appear in the voice and flats in the continuo; this alternation occurs continually in the Aria, which is in the key of B-flat minor. An extreme instance of the use of enharmonic change is seen in the voice part in bar 49, where the last three eighth-notes are actually notes of the same pitch, but are enharmonically written so as to appear otherwise at first. Needless to say, the effect of Marcello's eccentric notation is not evident to the ear of the listener; the notation is a sort of private joke between the performers, and is an example of what German scholars call *Augenmusik* ("eye music"). In the author's realization of the continuo the added smaller notes are always notated to follow the notes of the continuo in regard to the use of sharps or flats.

The notation is not the only "extravagance" in the piece, however. The first part of the da capo aria is in quintuple meter, which is so rare in the Baroque period as to be practically nonexistent. The only other contemporary use known to the author is in a small section of four bars within an aria of Handel's opera *Orlando* (Act II, Scene XI, p. 65 of the Handel Society Edition). Marcello handles the meter with grace and ease; the melody flows at all times very naturally and smoothly. In this section the composer has capriciously written the notes of the continuo in double the values of those in the voice part, and has used a proportional sign in bar 11 to indicate that the notes are to be played *alla breve* (that is, the half-note is to be considered as the beat, rather than the quarter-note) in order to correspond with the note values of the voice. Another extravagance is intended, perhaps, in the exuberant melisma on "-ra" of "vincera" (bars 28–31). In the middle section of the aria (bars 41–54) quadruple meter is resumed and maintained until the da capo return of the first section.

The parts of the text that precede and succeed the part of the cantata represented in Example 49 deal with the violent aspects of love—the extravagant speed with which it can plunge a lover from the heights to the depths, and the dangers of becoming a victim to its power and fury—which provide the composer with a motive for the musical extravagances in his setting. In the manuscript in which the cantata is extant the end of the text of the recitative is lacking (bar 10); the words in brackets represent a possible emendation which completes the meaning of the sentence and also rhymes with "lusinghiero" in the text. The text may be by Marcello, who was a man of letters as well as a composer. In the light of Example 49 it is not surprising that his most famous literary work is a satirical pamphlet entitled *Il teatro alla moda* ("The Opera alamode"; *ca.* 1720), a witty and amusing attack on the abuses suffered by the Italian opera. (Selections from this appear in *SR*, p. 518.)

The translation of the text:

*Recitative*

Love, thou art that cruel one that with fiery torch
Did'st reduce my heart to ashes.
But no! Never shall it be that an alluring face
Shall conquer me, now that my heart is free and proud.

*Aria*

As the furious wave dashes against the reef
  But does not break it,
So love assails my heart
  But will never again conquer it.
High and free my heart will always live,
For too dear to me is the joy of liberty.

Source: A manuscript in the Music Division of the New York Public Library, undated, but in a hand of the period in which the cantata was written.

## 49. Benedetto Marcello (1686–1739)
## "Amor tu sei,"
## *Stravaganze d'Amore*

Recitative
A - mor tu sei quell' Em - pio che con ar - den - te
fa - ce in - ce – ne - ri - sti del mio cor la
5
pa - ce, ma nò, non fia mai ve - ro, che

vol - to lu - sin - ghie - ro ab - bia di me la pal - ma
10
or che li - be-ro è il co - re e [al - ti - e - ro.]
Aria
Co - me l'on - da fu - ri - bon - da
ur - ta i sco - gli e non li fran - ge

15
ta - le a - mor fa guer-ra al cor, nè mai più lo vin- ce -
rà, nò ne mai più, nè mai più lo vin- ce -
rà.
20
Co - me l'on - da fu - ri -
bon - da ur - ta i sco - gli-e non li

fran - ge ta - le a- mor fa guer-ra al
25
cor, nè mai più lo vin - ce - rà, nò nè mai più,
nè mai più lo vin - ce - rà
30

ta- le a - mor fa guer-ra al
cor, nè mai più lo vin- ce - rà, nò nè mai più,
35
nè mai più lo vin- ce - rà, mai più, mai più, lo vin- ce-
rà.

40
[Fine]
Da un crine di-sciol-
to vi-vrà sem-pre il co-re per-chè trop-po m'è
45
ca-ro, trop-po m'è ca-ro go-der
la li-ber-tà. Da un crine di-sciol-

to vi - vrà sem - pre il cor, per - chè trop- po m'è
50
ca - ro, trop - po m'è ca - ro go - der
[Da Capo]
la li - ber - tà, go - der la li - - ber - tà.

# 50. Giovanni Battista Pergolesi Opera Buffa Recitative and Aria "Misero," from *Livietta e Tracollo*

The *opera buffa* as a type of opera distinct from *opera seria* arose in the early eighteenth century, when it became the custom to interpolate a humorous intermezzo in two acts as comic relief between the three acts of a serious opera. Act I of the intermezzo was given between the first and second acts of the opera, and Act II of the intermezzo between the second and third acts of the opera. It was for such a performance that the little comic opera *Livietta e Tracollo* was composed by Pergolesi, the first great master of the opera buffa. It was premiered at Naples in 1734, being performed between the acts of the same composer's *Adriano in Siria,* and was one of three such intermezzi written by Pergolesi during his tragically brief life—the others being *La Contadina astuta* (1734) and the epoch-making *La Serva Padrona* (1733).

The libretto of *Livietta e Tracollo,* by Mariani, is based on an absurd story of a rogue, Tracollo, who is caught stealing by one of his victims, Livietta, who threatens to deliver him to justice. Attempting to avoid being hanged, Tracollo pretends to be a mad astrologer, and so frightens Livietta with his dire predictions that she faints. Believing her dead, Tracollo is overcome with remorse, and confesses the love he had for her. When she recovers her senses, Livietta is so moved by his confession that she agrees to marry him if he will reform his ways. Example 50 occurs near the end of the first act, when Tracollo, threatened with arrest, is almost dead from fright at the prospect of a wretched death at the end of a rope; he gives vent to his feelings in a recitative and (da capo) aria that are masterpieces of humorous musical characterization.

The frantic despair of Tracollo keeps the scene at a high pitch throughout. Both recitative and aria begin without instrumental introduction; the rogue's cries to the forces of the underworld and of the heavens to witness his anguish are heightened by the use of an obbligato accompaniment in the recitative instead of the customary *secco* (Italian, "dry") harpsichord accompaniment. Harmony is used very sparingly until the last few bars of the recitative, the strings playing their expressive figure in octaves until then. During most of this intermezzo only three instruments are indicated—two violins and a bass, the basic trio sonata ensemble of the Baroque—a harpsichord continuo being understood. In some of the contemporaneous manuscripts, horns and oboes are specified for certain of the scenes, but not for this one.

The aria calls for vocalism of a high order. The range employed is over two octaves, from the *f* below the staff (in bar 25 and elsewhere) to the *g* above middle *c* (in bar 54). The melody is animated by many wide skips, including the unvocal but expressive drop of a major seventh (beginning of bar 45), and by rapid declamation of the word "povero" (bars 35 and 38), which heralds the patter singing later exploited so felicitously by Rossini. Pergolesi illustrates the text continually throughout the aria. The falling interval at each reference to the drop of the trap ("tracolar"—bars 25, 46, and 47), the broken figures when he sings of his "last sob" and his proximate departure from the world (bars 28–32), the quick drop through two octaves on the words "from head to foot" (bar 54), and the shuddering trills on the words "makes me shiver" (bars 57–58) underlined by the tremolo in the violins—these are only the more obvious instances of his imaginative ways of intensifying the sense of the text. In spite of the grotesquerie there is real terror in it; and though the eighteenth century was more callous about hanging than our own, Pergolesi's audience may have been glad to assure itself that this was a farce, and that Tracollo would somehow escape the noose.

The translation of the text:

*Recitative*

O wretched me! To whom shall I turn? Yes, to you, O Gods of Hades—Proserpine and Pluto—Hydras, Cerberuses, and Sphinxes;

Raging tempests, thunder and lightning, and you with your lengthy tails, O fateful comets—fixed stars and wandering planets, moons that wax and wane—
Stop in your courses to consider my tragic plight!

*Aria*

Here is poor Tracollo
Already close to the drop.
Already I see the noose around my neck,
Already I feel myself strangling!
Ah! . . . This is the last sob that comes
From my soul to my throat!
Already I have given up,
Ah! Already I am gone,
Already I see the noose around my neck!
Poor neck, poor Tracollo!
Poor, . . . poor neck,
This is your last sob!
Poor craw, poor throat, poor, . . . poor throat!
Already my soul has departed,
Already 'tis gone.

Already death is nigh me.
How ugly it is!
See with what a face it threatens me,
And chills me from head to foot,
And makes me shiver.

Source: *Tracollo, Intermède en deux actes de Signor Pergolesi*, p. 24. A French edition with Italian words, published in Paris, 1753.
Modern edition: F. Caffarelli, *G. B. Pergolesi, Opera Omnia, Vol. III, No. 11*, (*Il Teatro Comico*), Rome, 1941.

# 50. Giovanni Battista Pergolesi (1710–1736)

## "Misero," from *Livietta e Tracollo*

Recitative
Tracollo
Mi - se - ro! A chi mi vol - ge - rò?
Si, à vo - i, à voi, nu - mi d'a- ver - no,
Pro - ser-pi-ne e Plut-to - ni,

I - dre, Cer-be- ri sfin- gi,
tem-pes-to - se tem -
pes- te,
fol- go- ri, lam- pi e tuo- ni,
e voi che un pal - mo a- ve - te di co - da,
fu - ne - stis - si - me co - met - te,

15
stel- le fis-se-ed er-ran-ti,
lu- ne man-ca- ti, è
pie- ne,
fer-ma- te,
fer-ma-te il vo-stro cor-so,
à ri- mi-
20
rar
le mie tra- gi-che se-ne.
Aria
tr
Ec- co il po- ve- ro Tra-col- lo, già vi- ci- no à tra-co-
Sostenuto

25
lar. Già mi ve - do il lac- cio al col- lo, già mi sen - to sof - fo -
gar. Ah, Ah, Ah, Ah, que - st'è l'ul - ti - mo sin -
30
ghioz - zo giun - t'è l'al - ma al gar - ga - roz - zo. Già si par - te, già, già si
par - te, ah! già sen va, già sen

va. Già mi ve - do il lac - cio al col - lo. Po - ve - ro col - lo,
35
po - ve - ro Tra - col - lo! Po-ve- ro, po- ve-ro, po-ve-ro, po-ve- ro,
po- ve- ro, po- ve - ro col - lo. Que - st'è l'ul - ti - mo sin -
ghioz - zo. Po - ve - ro goz - zo! Po - ve - ro gar - ga -

roz - zo! Po-ve-ro, po-ve- ro, po- ve- ro, po-ve-ro, po-ve- ro, gar - ga-
40
roz-zo! Ec - co, che l'al-ma già si
par- te, già sen va, già sen va.
45
Ec - co il po - ve - ro Tra - col - lo, già vi - ci - no a tra - co -

lar, già vi - ci - no a tra - co - lar.
50
Fine
Già la mor - te mi si ac - co - sta, co - me è brut - ta, co - me è
brut - ta! Vi - di, vi - di con qual fac - cia mi mi - nac - cia, mi mi -

55
nac - cia, e da ca-po si- no a pie- di raf - fre - dar,
raf - fre - dar, tre - mar mi fa, tre - mar mi fa.
60
Aria D.C.

# Index

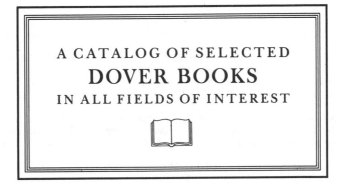

A CATALOG OF SELECTED

# DOVER BOOKS

IN ALL FIELDS OF INTEREST

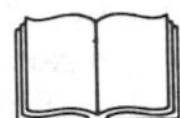

# A CATALOG OF SELECTED DOVER BOOKS IN ALL FIELDS OF INTEREST

CONCERNING THE SPIRITUAL IN ART, Wassily Kandinsky. Pioneering work by father of abstract art. Thoughts on color theory, nature of art. Analysis of earlier masters. 12 illustrations. 80pp. of text. 5⅜ x 8½. 23411-8 Pa. $4.95

ANIMALS: 1,419 Copyright-Free Illustrations of Mammals, Birds, Fish, Insects, etc., Jim Harter (ed.). Clear wood engravings present, in extremely lifelike poses, over 1,000 species of animals. One of the most extensive pictorial sourcebooks of its kind. Captions. Index. 284pp. 9 x 12. 23766-4 Pa. $14.95

CELTIC ART: The Methods of Construction, George Bain. Simple geometric techniques for making Celtic interlacements, spirals, Kells-type initials, animals, humans, etc. Over 500 illustrations. 160pp. 9 x 12. (USO) 22923-8 Pa. $9.95

AN ATLAS OF ANATOMY FOR ARTISTS, Fritz Schider. Most thorough reference work on art anatomy in the world. Hundreds of illustrations, including selections from works by Vesalius, Leonardo, Goya, Ingres, Michelangelo, others. 593 illustrations. 192pp. 7⅛ x 10¼. 20241-0 Pa. $9.95

CELTIC HAND STROKE-BY-STROKE (Irish Half-Uncial from "The Book of Kells"): An Arthur Baker Calligraphy Manual, Arthur Baker. Complete guide to creating each letter of the alphabet in distinctive Celtic manner. Covers hand position, strokes, pens, inks, paper, more. Illustrated. 48pp. 8¼ x 11. 24336-2 Pa. $3.95

EASY ORIGAMI, John Montroll. Charming collection of 32 projects (hat, cup, pelican, piano, swan, many more) specially designed for the novice origami hobbyist. Clearly illustrated easy-to-follow instructions insure that even beginning papercrafters will achieve successful results. 48pp. 8¼ x 11. 27298-2 Pa. $3.50

THE COMPLETE BOOK OF BIRDHOUSE CONSTRUCTION FOR WOODWORKERS, Scott D. Campbell. Detailed instructions, illustrations, tables. Also data on bird habitat and instinct patterns. Bibliography. 3 tables. 63 illustrations in 15 figures. 48pp. 5¼ x 8½. 24407-5 Pa. $2.50

BLOOMINGDALE'S ILLUSTRATED 1886 CATALOG: Fashions, Dry Goods and Housewares, Bloomingdale Brothers. Famed merchants' extremely rare catalog depicting about 1,700 products: clothing, housewares, firearms, dry goods, jewelry, more. Invaluable for dating, identifying vintage items. Also, copyright-free graphics for artists, designers. Co-published with Henry Ford Museum & Greenfield Village. 160pp. 8¼ x 11. 25780-0 Pa. $10.95

HISTORIC COSTUME IN PICTURES, Braun & Schneider. Over 1,450 costumed figures in clearly detailed engravings–from dawn of civilization to end of 19th century. Captions. Many folk costumes. 256pp. 8⅜ x 11¾. 23150-X Pa. $12.95

EARLY NINETEENTH-CENTURY CRAFTS AND TRADES, Peter Stockham (ed.). Extremely rare 1807 volume describes to youngsters the crafts and trades of the day: brickmaker, weaver, dressmaker, bookbinder, ropemaker, saddler, many more. Quaint prose, charming illustrations for each craft. 20 black-and-white line illustrations. 192pp. 4⅝ x 6. 27293-1 Pa. $4.95

VICTORIAN FASHIONS AND COSTUMES FROM HARPER'S BAZAR, 1867–1898, Stella Blum (ed.). Day costumes, evening wear, sports clothes, shoes, hats, other accessories in over 1,000 detailed engravings. 320pp. 9⅜ x 12¼. 22990-4 Pa. $15.95

GUSTAV STICKLEY, THE CRAFTSMAN, Mary Ann Smith. Superb study surveys broad scope of Stickley's achievement, especially in architecture. Design philosophy, rise and fall of the Craftsman empire, descriptions and floor plans for many Craftsman houses, more. 86 black-and-white halftones. 31 line illustrations. Introduction 208pp. 6½ x 9¼. 27210-9 Pa. $9.95

THE LONG ISLAND RAIL ROAD IN EARLY PHOTOGRAPHS, Ron Ziel. Over 220 rare photos, informative text document origin ( 1844) and development of rail service on Long Island. Vintage views of early trains, locomotives, stations, passengers, crews, much more. Captions. 8⅞ x 11¾. 26301-0 Pa. $13.95

THE BOOK OF OLD SHIPS: From Egyptian Galleys to Clipper Ships, Henry B. Culver. Superb, authoritative history of sailing vessels, with 80 magnificent line illustrations. Galley, bark, caravel, longship, whaler, many more. Detailed, informative text on each vessel by noted naval historian. Introduction. 256pp. 5⅜ x 8½. 27332-6 Pa. $7.95

TEN BOOKS ON ARCHITECTURE, Vitruvius. The most important book ever written on architecture. Early Roman aesthetics, technology, classical orders, site selection, all other aspects. Morgan translation. 331pp. 5⅜ x 8½. 20645-9 Pa. $8.95

THE HUMAN FIGURE IN MOTION, Eadweard Muybridge. More than 4,500 stopped-action photos, in action series, showing undraped men, women, children jumping, lying down, throwing, sitting, wrestling, carrying, etc. 390pp. 7⅞ x 10⅝. 20204-6 Clothbd. $27.95

TREES OF THE EASTERN AND CENTRAL UNITED STATES AND CANADA, William M. Harlow. Best one-volume guide to 140 trees. Full descriptions, woodlore, range, etc. Over 600 illustrations. Handy size. 288pp. 4½ x 6⅜. 20395-6 Pa. $6.95

SONGS OF WESTERN BIRDS, Dr. Donald J. Borror. Complete song and call repertoire of 60 western species, including flycatchers, juncoes, cactus wrens, many more–includes fully illustrated booklet. Cassette and manual 99913-0 $8.95

GROWING AND USING HERBS AND SPICES, Milo Miloradovich. Versatile handbook provides all the information needed for cultivation and use of all the herbs and spices available in North America. 4 illustrations. Index. Glossary. 236pp. 5⅜ x 8½. 25058-X Pa. $7.95

BIG BOOK OF MAZES AND LABYRINTHS, Walter Shepherd. 50 mazes and labyrinths in all–classical, solid, ripple, and more–in one great volume. Perfect inexpensive puzzler for clever youngsters. Full solutions. 112pp. 8⅛ x 11. 22951-3 Pa. $4.95

ANATOMY: A Complete Guide for Artists, Joseph Sheppard. A master of figure drawing shows artists how to render human anatomy convincingly. Over 460 illustrations. 224pp. 8⅜ x 11¼. 27279-6 Pa. $11.95

MEDIEVAL CALLIGRAPHY: Its History and Technique, Marc Drogin. Spirited history, comprehensive instruction manual covers 13 styles (ca. 4th century thru 15th). Excellent photographs; directions for duplicating medieval techniques with modern tools. 224pp. 8⅜ x 11¼. 26142-5 Pa. $12.95

DRIED FLOWERS: How to Prepare Them, Sarah Whitlock and Martha Rankin. Complete instructions on how to use silica gel, meal and borax, perlite aggregate, sand and borax, glycerine and water to create attractive permanent flower arrangements. 12 illustrations. 32pp. 5⅜ x 8½. 21802-3 Pa. $1.00

EASY-TO-MAKE BIRD FEEDERS FOR WOODWORKERS, Scott D. Campbell. Detailed, simple-to-use guide for designing, constructing, caring for and using feeders. Text, illustrations for 12 classic and contemporary designs. 96pp. 5⅜ x 8½. 25847-5 Pa. $3.95

SCOTTISH WONDER TALES FROM MYTH AND LEGEND, Donald A. Mackenzie. 16 lively tales tell of giants rumbling down mountainsides, of a magic wand that turns stone pillars into warriors, of gods and goddesses, evil hags, powerful forces and more. 240pp. 5⅜ x 8½. 29677-6 Pa. $6.95

THE HISTORY OF UNDERCLOTHES, C. Willett Cunnington and Phyllis Cunnington. Fascinating, well-documented survey covering six centuries of English undergarments, enhanced with over 100 illustrations: 12th-century laced-up bodice, footed long drawers (1795), 19th-century bustles, 19th-century corsets for men, Victorian "bust improvers," much more. 272pp. 5⅜ x 8¼. 27124-2 Pa. $9.95

ARTS AND CRAFTS FURNITURE: The Complete Brooks Catalog of 1912, Brooks Manufacturing Co. Photos and detailed descriptions of more than 150 now very collectible furniture designs from the Arts and Crafts movement depict davenports, settees, buffets, desks, tables, chairs, bedsteads, dressers and more, all built of solid, quarter-sawed oak. Invaluable for students and enthusiasts of antiques, Americana and the decorative arts. 80pp. 6½ x 9¼. 27471-3 Pa. $8.95

HOW WE INVENTED THE AIRPLANE: An Illustrated History, Orville Wright. Fascinating firsthand account covers early experiments, construction of planes and motors, first flights, much more. Introduction and commentary by Fred C. Kelly. 76 photographs. 96pp. 8¼ x 11. 25662-6 Pa. $8.95

THE ARTS OF THE SAILOR: Knotting, Splicing and Ropework, Hervey Garrett Smith. Indispensable shipboard reference covers tools, basic knots and useful hitches; handsewing and canvas work, more. Over 100 illustrations. Delightful reading for sea lovers. 256pp. 5⅜ x 8½. 26440-8 Pa. $8.95

FRANK LLOYD WRIGHT'S FALLINGWATER: The House and Its History, Second, Revised Edition, Donald Hoffmann. A total revision–both in text and illustrations–of the standard document on Fallingwater, the boldest, most personal architectural statement of Wright's mature years, updated with valuable new material from the recently opened Frank Lloyd Wright Archives. "Fascinating"–*The New York Times*. 116 illustrations. 128pp. 9¼ x 10¾. 27430-6 Pa. $12.95

PHOTOGRAPHIC SKETCHBOOK OF THE CIVIL WAR, Alexander Gardner. 100 photos taken on field during the Civil War. Famous shots of Manassas Harper's Ferry, Lincoln, Richmond, slave pens, etc. 244pp. 10⅝ x 8¼. 22731-6 Pa. $10.95

FIVE ACRES AND INDEPENDENCE, Maurice G. Kains. Great back-to-the-land classic explains basics of self-sufficient farming. The one book to get. 95 illustrations. 397pp. 5⅜ x 8½. 20974-1 Pa. $7.95

SONGS OF EASTERN BIRDS, Dr. Donald J. Borror. Songs and calls of 60 species most common to eastern U.S.: warblers, woodpeckers, flycatchers, thrushes, larks, many more in high-quality recording. Cassette and manual 99912-2 $9.95

A MODERN HERBAL, Margaret Grieve. Much the fullest, most exact, most useful compilation of herbal material. Gigantic alphabetical encyclopedia, from aconite to zedoary, gives botanical information, medical properties, folklore, economic uses, much else. Indispensable to serious reader. 161 illustrations. 888pp. 6½ x 9¼. 2-vol. set. (USO) Vol. I: 22798-7 Pa. $9.95
Vol. II: 22799-5 Pa. $9.95

HIDDEN TREASURE MAZE BOOK, Dave Phillips. Solve 34 challenging mazes accompanied by heroic tales of adventure. Evil dragons, people-eating plants, blood-thirsty giants, many more dangerous adversaries lurk at every twist and turn. 34 mazes, stories, solutions. 48pp. 8¼ x 11. 24566-7 Pa. $2.95

LETTERS OF W. A. MOZART, Wolfgang A. Mozart. Remarkable letters show bawdy wit, humor, imagination, musical insights, contemporary musical world; includes some letters from Leopold Mozart. 276pp. 5⅜ x 8½. 22859-2 Pa. $7.95

BASIC PRINCIPLES OF CLASSICAL BALLET, Agrippina Vaganova. Great Russian theoretician, teacher explains methods for teaching classical ballet. 118 illustrations. 175pp. 5⅜ x 8½. 22036-2 Pa. $5.95

THE JUMPING FROG, Mark Twain. Revenge edition. The original story of The Celebrated Jumping Frog of Calaveras County, a hapless French translation, and Twain's hilarious "retranslation" from the French. 12 illustrations. 66pp. 5⅜ x 8½.
22686-7 Pa. $3.95

BEST REMEMBERED POEMS, Martin Gardner (ed.). The 126 poems in this superb collection of 19th- and 20th-century British and American verse range from Shelley's "To a Skylark" to the impassioned "Renascence" of Edna St. Vincent Millay and to Edward Lear's whimsical "The Owl and the Pussycat." 224pp. 5⅜ x 8½.
27165-X Pa. $5.95

COMPLETE SONNETS, William Shakespeare. Over 150 exquisite poems deal with love, friendship, the tyranny of time, beauty's evanescence, death and other themes in language of remarkable power, precision and beauty. Glossary of archaic terms. 80pp. $5\frac{3}{16}$ x 8¼. 26686-9 Pa. $1.00

BODIES IN A BOOKSHOP, R. T. Campbell. Challenging mystery of blackmail and murder with ingenious plot and superbly drawn characters. In the best tradition of British suspense fiction. 192pp. 5⅜ x 8½. 24720-1 Pa. $6.95

THE WIT AND HUMOR OF OSCAR WILDE, Alvin Redman (ed.). More than 1,000 ripostes, paradoxes, wisecracks: Work is the curse of the drinking classes; I can resist everything except temptation; etc. 258pp. 5⅜ x 8½. 20602-5 Pa. $6.95

SHAKESPEARE LEXICON AND QUOTATION DICTIONARY, Alexander Schmidt. Full definitions, locations, shades of meaning in every word in plays and poems. More than 50,000 exact quotations. 1,485pp. 6½ x 9¼. 2-vol. set.
Vol. 1: 22726-X Pa. $17.95
Vol. 2: 22727-8 Pa. $17.95

SELECTED POEMS, Emily Dickinson. Over 100 best-known, best-loved poems by one of America's foremost poets, reprinted from authoritative early editions. No comparable edition at this price. Index of first lines. 64pp. 5$\frac{3}{16}$ x 8¼.
26466-1 Pa. $1.00

CELEBRATED CASES OF JUDGE DEE (DEE GOONG AN), translated by Robert van Gulik. Authentic 18th-century Chinese detective novel; Dee and associates solve three interlocked cases. Led to van Gulik's own stories with same characters. Extensive introduction. 9 illustrations. 237pp. 5⅜ x 8½. 23337-5 Pa. $7.95

THE MALLEUS MALEFICARUM OF KRAMER AND SPRENGER, translated by Montague Summers. Full text of most important witchhunter's "bible," used by both Catholics and Protestants. 278pp. 6⅝ x 10. 22802-9 Pa. $12.95

SPANISH STORIES/CUENTOS ESPAÑOLES: A Dual-Language Book, Angel Flores (ed.). Unique format offers 13 great stories in Spanish by Cervantes, Borges, others. Faithful English translations on facing pages. 352pp. 5⅜ x 8½.
25399-6 Pa. $8.95

THE CHICAGO WORLD'S FAIR OF 1893: A Photographic Record, Stanley Appelbaum (ed.). 128 rare photos show 200 buildings, Beaux-Arts architecture, Midway, original Ferris Wheel, Edison's kinetoscope, more. Architectural emphasis; full text. 116pp. 8¼ x 11. 23990-X Pa. $9.95

OLD QUEENS, N.Y., IN EARLY PHOTOGRAPHS, Vincent F. Seyfried and William Asadorian. Over 160 rare photographs of Maspeth, Jamaica, Jackson Heights, and other areas. Vintage views of DeWitt Clinton mansion, 1939 World's Fair and more. Captions. 192pp. 8⅞ x 11. 26358-4 Pa. $12.95

CAPTURED BY THE INDIANS: 15 Firsthand Accounts, 1750-1870, Frederick Drimmer. Astounding true historical accounts of grisly torture, bloody conflicts, relentless pursuits, miraculous escapes and more, by people who lived to tell the tale. 384pp. 5⅜ x 8½. 24901-8 Pa. $8.95

THE WORLD'S GREAT SPEECHES, Lewis Copeland and Lawrence W. Lamm (eds.). Vast collection of 278 speeches of Greeks to 1970. Powerful and effective models; unique look at history. 842pp. 5⅜ x 8½. 20468-5 Pa. $14.95

THE BOOK OF THE SWORD, Sir Richard F. Burton. Great Victorian scholar/adventurer's eloquent, erudite history of the "queen of weapons"–from prehistory to early Roman Empire. Evolution and development of early swords, variations (sabre, broadsword, cutlass, scimitar, etc.), much more. 336pp. 6⅛ x 9¼.
25434-8 Pa. $9.95

AUTOBIOGRAPHY: The Story of My Experiments with Truth, Mohandas K. Gandhi. Boyhood, legal studies, purification, the growth of the Satyagraha (nonviolent protest) movement. Critical, inspiring work of the man responsible for the freedom of India. 480pp. 5⅜ x 8½. (USO) 24593-4 Pa. $8.95

CELTIC MYTHS AND LEGENDS, T. W. Rolleston. Masterful retelling of Irish and Welsh stories and tales. Cuchulain, King Arthur, Deirdre, the Grail, many more. First paperback edition. 58 full-page illustrations. 512pp. 5⅜ x 8½. 26507-2 Pa. $9.95

THE PRINCIPLES OF PSYCHOLOGY, William James. Famous long course complete, unabridged. Stream of thought, time perception, memory, experimental methods; great work decades ahead of its time. 94 figures. 1,391pp. 5⅜ x 8½. 2-vol. set.
Vol. I: 20381-6 Pa. $13.95
Vol. II: 20382-4 Pa. $14.95

THE WORLD AS WILL AND REPRESENTATION, Arthur Schopenhauer. Definitive English translation of Schopenhauer's life work, correcting more than 1,000 errors, omissions in earlier translations. Translated by E. F. J. Payne. Total of 1,269pp. 5⅜ x 8½. 2-vol. set. Vol. 1: 21761-2 Pa. $12.95
Vol. 2: 21762-0 Pa. $12.95

MAGIC AND MYSTERY IN TIBET, Madame Alexandra David-Neel. Experiences among lamas, magicians, sages, sorcerers, Bonpa wizards. A true psychic discovery. 32 illustrations. 321pp. 5⅜ x 8½. (USO) 22682-4 Pa. $9.95

THE EGYPTIAN BOOK OF THE DEAD, E. A. Wallis Budge. Complete reproduction of Ani's papyrus, finest ever found. Full hieroglyphic text, interlinear transliteration, word-for-word translation, smooth translation. 533pp. 6½ x 9¼.
21866-X Pa. $11.95

MATHEMATICS FOR THE NONMATHEMATICIAN, Morris Kline. Detailed, college-level treatment of mathematics in cultural and historical context, with numerous exercises. Recommended Reading Lists. Tables. Numerous figures. 641pp. 5⅜ x 8½.
24823-2 Pa. $11.95

THEORY OF WING SECTIONS: Including a Summary of Airfoil Data, Ira H. Abbott and A. E. von Doenhoff. Concise compilation of subsonic aerodynamic characteristics of NACA wing sections, plus description of theory. 350pp. of tables. 693pp. 5⅜ x 8½. 60586-8 Pa. $14.95

THE RIME OF THE ANCIENT MARINER, Gustave Doré, S. T. Coleridge. Doré's finest work; 34 plates capture moods, subtleties of poem. Flawless full-size reproductions printed on facing pages with authoritative text of poem. "Beautiful. Simply beautiful."–*Publisher's Weekly*. 77pp. 9¼ x 12. 22305-1 Pa. $7.95

NORTH AMERICAN INDIAN DESIGNS FOR ARTISTS AND CRAFTSPEOPLE, Eva Wilson. Over 360 authentic copyright-free designs adapted from Navajo blankets, Hopi pottery, Sioux buffalo hides, more. Geometrics, symbolic figures, plant and animal motifs, etc. 128pp. 8⅜ x 11. (EUK) 25341-4 Pa. $8.95

SCULPTURE: Principles and Practice, Louis Slobodkin. Step-by-step approach to clay, plaster, metals, stone; classical and modern. 253 drawings, photos. 255pp. 8⅛ x 11.
22960-2 Pa. $11.95

*CATALOG OF DOVER BOOKS*

THE INFLUENCE OF SEA POWER UPON HISTORY, 1660–1783, A. T. Mahan. Influential classic of naval history and tactics still used as text in war colleges. First paperback edition. 4 maps. 24 battle plans. 640pp. 5⅜ x 8½. 25509-3 Pa. $14.95

THE STORY OF THE TITANIC AS TOLD BY ITS SURVIVORS, Jack Winocour (ed.). What it was really like. Panic, despair, shocking inefficiency, and a little heroism. More thrilling than any fictional account. 26 illustrations. 320pp. 5⅜ x 8½. 20610-6 Pa. $8.95

FAIRY AND FOLK TALES OF THE IRISH PEASANTRY, William Butler Yeats (ed.). Treasury of 64 tales from the twilight world of Celtic myth and legend: "The Soul Cages," "The Kildare Pooka," "King O'Toole and his Goose," many more. Introduction and Notes by W. B. Yeats. 352pp. 5⅜ x 8½. 26941-8 Pa. $8.95

BUDDHIST MAHAYANA TEXTS, E. B. Cowell and Others (eds.). Superb, accurate translations of basic documents in Mahayana Buddhism, highly important in history of religions. The Buddha-karita of Asvaghosha, Larger Sukhavativyuha, more. 448pp. 5⅜ x 8½. 25552-2 Pa. $12.95

ONE TWO THREE . . . INFINITY: Facts and Speculations of Science, George Gamow. Great physicist's fascinating, readable overview of contemporary science: number theory, relativity, fourth dimension, entropy, genes, atomic structure, much more. 128 illustrations. Index. 352pp. 5⅜ x 8½. 25664-2 Pa. $8.95

ENGINEERING IN HISTORY, Richard Shelton Kirby, et al. Broad, nontechnical survey of history's major technological advances: birth of Greek science, industrial revolution, electricity and applied science, 20th-century automation, much more. 181 illustrations. ". . . excellent . . ."–*Isis*. Bibliography. vii + 530pp. 5⅜ x 8¼. 26412-2 Pa. $14.95

DALÍ ON MODERN ART: The Cuckolds of Antiquated Modern Art, Salvador Dalí. Influential painter skewers modern art and its practitioners. Outrageous evaluations of Picasso, Cézanne, Turner, more. 15 renderings of paintings discussed. 44 calligraphic decorations by Dalí. 96pp. 5⅜ x 8½. (USO) 29220-7 Pa. $4.95

ANTIQUE PLAYING CARDS: A Pictorial History, Henry René D'Allemagne. Over 900 elaborate, decorative images from rare playing cards (14th–20th centuries): Bacchus, death, dancing dogs, hunting scenes, royal coats of arms, players cheating, much more. 96pp. 9¼ x 12¼. 29265-7 Pa. $12.95

MAKING FURNITURE MASTERPIECES: 30 Projects with Measured Drawings, Franklin H. Gottshall. Step-by-step instructions, illustrations for constructing handsome, useful pieces, among them a Sheraton desk, Chippendale chair, Spanish desk, Queen Anne table and a William and Mary dressing mirror. 224pp. 8⅛ x 11¼. 29338-6 Pa. $13.95

THE FOSSIL BOOK: A Record of Prehistoric Life, Patricia V. Rich et al. Profusely illustrated definitive guide covers everything from single-celled organisms and dinosaurs to birds and mammals and the interplay between climate and man. Over 1,500 illustrations. 760pp. 7½ x 10⅛. 29371-8 Pa. $29.95

*Prices subject to change without notice.*

Available at your book dealer or write for free catalog to Dept. GI, Dover Publications, Inc., 31 East 2nd St., Mineola, N.Y. 11501. Dover publishes more than 500 books each year on science, elementary and advanced mathematics, biology, music, art, literary history, social sciences and other areas.